HOW TO MANAGE
CORPORATE
CASH
EFFECTIVELY

HOW TO MANAGE

CORPORATE

CASH

EFFECTIVELY

JOSEPH E. FINNERTY

amacom

American Management Association

This book is available at a special
discount when ordered in bulk quantities.
For information, contact Special Sales Department,
AMACOM, a division of American Management Association,
135 West 50th Street, New York, NY   10020.

This publication is designed to provide accurate and authoritative information in regard to the subject matter covered. It is sold with the understanding that the publisher is not engaged in rendering legal, accounting,
or other professional service. If legal advice or other expert assistance is
required, the services of a competent professional person should be sought.

3 2280 00495 7189

Library of Congress Cataloging-in-Publication Data

Finnerty, Joseph E.
      How to manage corporate cash effectively/Joseph E. Finnerty.
            p. cm.
      Includes bibliographical references and index.
      ISBN 0-8144-7717-8 (comb bound)
      1. Corporations—United States—France.   2. Cash management—
United States.   3. Cash management.   4. Cash flow.   I. Title.
HG4028.C45F54   1991
658.15′244—dc20   90-56409
                                                                              CIP

Printing number

10   9   8   7   6   5   4   3   2   1

To
Sandy, Matt, and **Dan,**
my own extremely complex cash flow problem.

CONTENTS

PREFACE

Managing a company's cash flow, if done correctly, goes unnoticed as a necessary job that must be done. If done incorrectly, all other activities of the company will be affected even to the extent of the company going bankrupt. Coupled with a changing financial environment, advances in communications, increasing accessibility of computer hardware and software, and deregulation of the financial system, the management of corporate cash has increased in importance as well as becoming more difficult and complex.

Many of the developments taking place today are the result of increasing competition among financial institutions, a large number of failures of financial institutions, an increase in the turbulence in financial markets, and an increase in the sophistication of corporate cash managers. The purpose of *How to Manage Corporate Cash Effectively* is to provide a framework upon which each individual cash manager can structure an approach to his company's unique cash flow problems. Additionally, descriptive material dealing with financial markets, financial instruments, and computer-based financial systems is provided so that the manager can develop a sense of the environment within which he must operate.

The first two chapters establish a foundation of what working capital is and what cash flow is. How are these two concepts related? How are they different?

Chapters 3 and 4 introduce the ideas of planning and forecasting, and how these techniques can be applied to cash flow management. Regardless of the degree of complexity or simplicity of the organization in which the cash flow manager operates, these techniques will provide the groundwork and information that will be necessary for managing a company's cash flow.

Chapter 5, "Cash Mobilization Techniques," deals with the internal flows or systems within the company. Chapter 6 describes one of the major linkages to the outside financial system, a bank. Through this institution, the financial markets are linked to the internal systems of the company. Therefore, maintaining a good banking relationship is paramount to the success of a company's cash management program.

Chapters 7, 8, 9, and 10 provide a further look at the external environment in which the cash manager must operate, both domestically and internationally.

It is hoped that both the old veteran and the inexperienced rookie can gain some appreciation for the techniques and environment of cash flow management offered in this book.

Joseph E. Finnerty, Ph.D.
Champaign, Illinois

HOW TO MANAGE

CORPORATE

CASH

EFFECTIVELY

Chapter 1

Fundamentals of Corporate Cash Management

By the end of this chapter, the reader will be able to:

Learning Objectives

1. List at least five functions of the cash manager.
2. Describe the flow of funds through the corporation.
3. Discuss the basic concepts of cash management.
4. Compare the treasurer's duties to a cash manager's direct responsibilities.

Corporate cash includes all the money a corporation owns. Corporations usually keep most of their money in checking accounts at banks, although a small amount of actual currency is kept in the office for minor purchases (petty cash). Most corporations also own longer-term bank accounts and marketable securities, and these are closely related to cash. Marketable securities are bonds, stocks, and other securities that a company buys in order to earn interest on its money. Marketable securities are easily traded (marketable) and can be converted to cash quickly when necessary. In fact, a company's balance sheet may show cash and marketable securities added together on a single line under assets.

To manage this cash wisely, it is necessary to know exactly how cash is used and how it is related to accounts receivable, inventory, payables, and all other short-term assets and liabilities. In other words, to effectively manage a company's cash, the cash manager must understand the whole structure of working capital in the corporation. In addition, longer-term uses of cash such as investment in capital budgeting projects, the payment of dividends, and taxes and principal and interest on long-term debts also affect the needs and uses of cash flow. To be most effective, the cash manager needs to see exactly how working capital relates to the corporation's long-term investment and financial structure. This in turn requires an understanding of the corporation's long-term goals.

So, while learning to do the best possible job in managing a corporation's day-to-day cash transactions, a cash manager will also be contributing to the long-run stability and profitability of the corporation.

➤ Functions and Importance
of Cash Management

Cash management can be divided into four functions: cash forecasting and planning, cash mobilization, banks and other short-term cash sources, and surplus cash investing. We discuss each of these categories in detail in later chapters.

The skill with which you manage your company's cash directly affects corporate strength and health. The more effective your corporate cash management program, the more you help your company survive business downturns, take advantage of new opportunities during prosperous times, and earn higher profits at all times.

Here is an imaginary case history that illustrates these points. Many years ago, a small group of engineers started a new company to manufacture airplanes. At about the same time, in a neighboring state, a similar group founded a competing company. Both companies had problems at first, but they survived the rough early years; when flying became big business, they both prospered. Soon they were building passenger planes for many of the world's airlines, fighter planes for the U.S. Department of Defense, and even rockets to travel to the moon and Mars.

Here are figures from a recent income statement:

	Company A	Company B
Sales (in millions of dollars)	$1,500	$1,500
Earnings (in millions of dollars)	91	92

Sales are equal, and earnings are almost exactly the same at about 6 percent of sales. Although the income statements for the two companies look quite similar, the balance sheets are very different. Here are some selected items from the balance sheets:

	Company A	Company B
Cash (in millions of dollars)	$ 20	$ 80
Marketable securities (in millions of dollars)	20	80
Accounts receivable (in millions of dollars)	400	150
Inventory (in millions of dollars)	400	150
Accounts payable (in millions of dollars)	200	300

A comparison of their balance sheets shows significant differences. Company B is holding more cash and marketable securities (near cash). Company A, on the other hand, is holding substantially more of its assets in accounts receivable and inventory. On the liability side, Company B has more accounts payable than Company A.

Without more information, it is impossible to tell which company is in better shape or what the correct levels of cash, accounts receivable, and inventories should be. However, in this case, Company A turned out to be dangerously low in cash, with too much of its money tied up in accounts receivable and inventory. When the business cycle turned down and a small recession began, Company A's customers paid their bills more slowly.

Company A was unable to convert its $400 million of accounts receivable into cash as quickly as it had planned. Furthermore, these same customers slowed down their purchases of new equipment, so Company A was not able to convert its inventory into cash quickly either. Cash outflows, such as payrolls and taxes, continued at their usual high levels, quickly using up Company A's small cash account. They had very few marketable securities to fall back on, and the company found itself in a cash squeeze. An emergency loan, arranged quickly and on unfavorable terms, was needed to save Company A.

Meanwhile, Company B experienced the same business downturn. Its customers slowed down their payments of past bills and sharply reduced their new purchases. Company B, however, had less money tied up in accounts receivable and inventory, so these slowdowns did not hurt Company B as much as they did Company A. What's more, Company B had healthy reserves of cash and marketable securities, and this cash planning paid off. Although Company B did have to use its cash reserves during the recession, it stayed a safe distance away from bankruptcy and never had to arrange emergency loans.

The ability to weather a downturn in business is just one of the advantages of careful cash management. Another advantage is the ability to exploit opportunities fully in times of prosperity. For example, if the economy had turned sharply up instead of down in the above case, Company B might have also been in a stronger position. If a new customer had demanded long-term credit before placing an order, Company B (with fewer accounts receivable) would have been better able to extend this credit and make the sale.

In either bad times or good times, Company B will earn additional profits from its investments. Company B has $80 million invested in interest-bearing marketable securities compared to Company A's $20 million. These securities are a continuing source of extra income and profit. It also shows that cash management on a day-to-day basis directly impacts on all other aspects of the company's business operations, credit standing, profitability, and growth.

➤ CASH MANAGEMENT AND THE PRINCIPLES OF MODERN FINANCE

Two of the most often cited principles of modern finance are as follows:

1. Management should maximize the value of shareholder wealth.
2. Management's decisions should be based upon the maximization of the net present value of the risk-adjusted cash flow.

In most privately held organizations, the owners or shareholders usually take an active role in managing the company. Therefore, it is not very difficult to see a direct relationship between owner-management decisions and the wealth of these owner-managers. For publicly traded companies, where ownership and management are separated, the link between management decisions and shareholder wealth may be somewhat obscure. However, we have only to look to the merger and takeover wave of the 1980s to see the importance of this relationship. If the management is acting in the best interest of shareholders—that is, if it is maximizing their wealth—then it would be very difficult for outside interests to offer the owners a better price for their shares because management is already doing all that can be done. Likewise, shareholders who perceive that their shares are fairly priced because of management action are less likely to sell them to outside interests.

To put the principle of shareholder wealth maximization into practice, management must understand the link between cash flow, share price, and shareholder wealth. There is considerable evidence that the market places a high value on a company's cash flow. Therefore, in order to maximize share price (shareholder wealth), cash flow should be managed effectively by a company's decision makers. Two questions regarding cash flow are worth asking at this time; (1) When is the cash flow actually available for company use, and (2) How risky are the prospective cash flows that the company may have available in the future?

One principle of modern finance says to maximize the net present value of a company's cash flow that is subject to risk. A simple net present value (NPV) model can be used to show how this can be operationalized, that is, made to work in the real world.

$$NPV = - \text{Cost} + \sum_{t=1}^{n} \frac{\text{Cash flow after tax}_t}{(1 + RAD)^t}$$

where:

       RAD is the risk-adjusted discount rate.
       t is the time at which the cash flow occurs.
       n is the last period in time when the cash flow will occur.

What management needs to do is to forecast, plan, budget, and manage the cash flow component of the NPV model while considering the timing and riskiness of the various cash flows. If its decisions can maximize the NPV, then the price of the company's securities will go up and the wealth of shareholders will be increased. In the remainder of this book, we will focus on those short-term management decisions that affect cash flow, keeping in mind the interrelationship between those cash flows and the company's long-run structure. An evaluation of the risk and timing of the cash flows will be required in order to ensure that the short-run working capital decisions are in concert with a company's long-run viability.

➢ CASH AND WORKING CAPITAL

Cash is part of working capital. It is, however, only *one* part and is not synonymous with working capital. To be specific, working capital is usu-

	DOLLARS	PERCENTAGE
Cash	$ 15	5%
Marketable securities	15	5
Accounts receivable	120	40
Inventories	120	40
Other current assets	30	10
Total Current Assets (CA)	$300	100%
Notes and payables	110	55%
Other current liabilities	90	45
Total Current Liabilities (CL)	$200	100%
Net working capital (CA – CL)	$100	

$$\text{Current ratio} \left(\frac{\text{Current assets}}{\text{Current liabilities}} \right) \quad \frac{\$300}{\$200} = 1.5$$

EXHIBIT 1–1   CURRENT ASSETS AND LIABILITIES ON THE BALANCE SHEET

ally defined as a company's current assets, or those items listed as current assets on a company's balance sheet. These include cash, marketable securities, accounts receivable, and inventory. Each of these items is either cash, readily converted into cash (marketable securities), or able to be converted into cash in the course of the company's normal operations in a year or less (accounts receivable and inventory).

Although all these items compose working capital, we also speak of *net working capital*. Net working capital consists of a firm's current assets minus its current liabilities. These current liabilities include accounts payable, wages and salaries payable, taxes payable, and bank loans (due in a year or less). Net working capital presents a truer, but harsher, picture of a firm's financial strength by showing how much money would be available if all short-term assets were converted to cash and all short-term liabilities were paid off.

Exhibit 1–1 shows the balance sheet for a typical manufacturing company. Because most companies have more current assets than current liabilities, the net working capital figure is usually positive (or the current ratio is above 1). The actual structure and relationships between current assets and current liabilities will vary from company to company or from industry to industry. For example, service organizations generally have few or no inventories, and banks or other financial institutions usually hold larger amounts of cash. The financial structure of a company's liabilities will also vary, with different mixes of short-term and long-term debt and, within the short-term liabilities section, different types of financing instruments.

A major problem with just looking at a balance sheet is that it represents a company's financial position at one point in time only. Earlier we indicated that management should be interested in cash flow. We can develop an appreciation for the concept of cash flow by looking at circulating working capital. The term *circulating working capital* refers to the fact

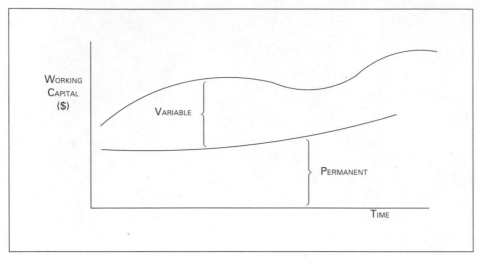

Exhibit 1–2   Permanent and Variable Working Capital

that the accounting value represented by the various short-term asset and liability accounts changes over time. For example: A company might use cash to purchase inventory, which is converted into a saleable product. This product is sold on account, thereby creating an account receivable that ultimately will be collected, giving the company more cash. While this process is going on, the company is incurring obligations to suppliers and workers, thereby increasing accounts payable, which ultimately must be paid off in cash.

Another way of looking at working capital, or more precisely a company's circulating working capital, is to divide the level of working capital over time into two components. The first can be viewed as permanent working capital. That is, over any period of time—a day, month, year, or business cycle—none of the accounts of cash, accounts receivable, inventory, or payables ever falls below a certain level. On a continuing basis there is always *some* value tied up in each of the accounts. That value is called permanent working capital (it should be noted that as a company grows over time, the level of permanent working capital increases). The second component of working capital over time is a transitory one, called variable working capital. This component reflects the period-to-period increases or decreases in the amount of working capital caused by seasonal or cyclical fluctuations. Exhibit 1–2 shows how these two components of working capital change over time.

Later on in Chapter 4, when we address the problem of forecasting cash flows, we consider this idea of permanent and variable working capital. For now, the next step in our development of the concept of working capital is to introduce the idea of the flow of funds through a corporation.

➤ Flow of Funds

Flow of funds, or the movement among changing assets, liabilities, revenues, and expenses, encompasses all segments of the corporation and is

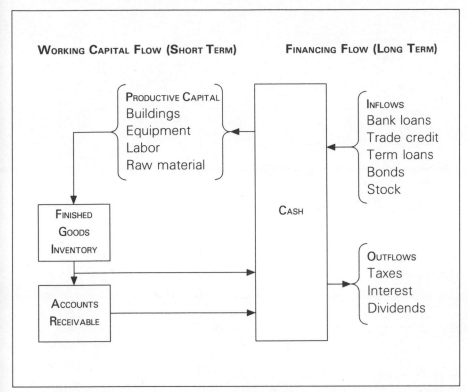

WORKING CAPITAL FLOW (SHORT TERM)   **FINANCING FLOW (LONG TERM)**

PRODUCTIVE CAPITAL
Buildings
Equipment
Labor
Raw material

FINISHED
GOODS
INVENTORY

ACCOUNTS
RECEIVABLE

CASH

INFLOWS
Bank loans
Trade credit
Term loans
Bonds
Stock

OUTFLOWS
Taxes
Interest
Dividends

EXHIBIT 1–3   FLOW OF FUNDS

related to most important decisions. However, not all funds flows involve cash. For example, changes in noncash expenses (that is, depreciation) or changes resulting from accrual accounting methods do not necessarily coincide with cash. Exhibit 1–3 shows this basic flow of funds. Because the flow is circular and continuous, it is possible to start anywhere in the chain shown in Exhibit 1–3. For example, if you start with inventory, you will see that sales to customers convert the inventory into accounts receivable—that is, the company ships an item from inventory to a customer and also sends a bill. When the customer pays the bill, the account receivable is turned into cash. The company can then use this cash for any long-term or short-term corporate purpose.

The basic flow of funds for any company follows this pattern. Of course, the actual situation is much more complex. For example, some sales to customers might be for cash and would therefore bypass accounts receivable. And, of course, cash is not just spent for the purchase of more goods; it must also be used for wages, rent, taxes, dividends, and so on. The principle of cash management has historically been to speed up the inflow of funds and to slow down the outflow. However, cash managers today are much more concerned about cash synchronization. This is an important concept that we will address in greater detail in Chapter 5.

Another important concept in the area of cash management is liquidity, which refers to how quickly an asset can be converted to cash without a significant loss to fair market value. The more liquid an asset, the faster the conversion and the smaller the loss to fair market value. Clearly, cash is the most liquid of all assets. Near-cash assets such as marketable securities are also very liquid and can be converted to cash usually in a day or two.

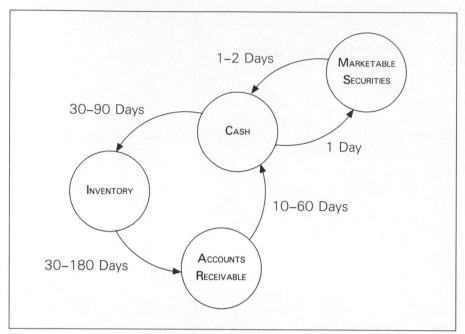

EXHIBIT 1–4   TIME DELAYS IN THE FLOW OF WORKING CAPITAL

Accounts receivables are less liquid. Normally, accounts receivables are outstanding an average of 30 days. If money is tight, that 30-day collection period may increase to 60 days or longer. On the other hand, if the firm adopts a vigorous collection policy and employs efficient collection procedures, the 30-day average may be reduced to considerably fewer days. In either event, management needs to be careful in monitoring sales and profit levels. A too lenient policy may require additional borrowing and higher bad debt costs, whereas a too stringent policy may impede sales growth, harm customer goodwill, or both.

Inventory is even less liquid. This is because inventory must first be sold to a customer (that is, converted to an account receivable), and then the account receivable must be collected. A company may hold an item in inventory for months before selling it to a customer. Many companies must tie up a large fraction of their working capital in inventory.

Time delays strongly affect how a company uses its working capital. If a company ties up a great deal of money in inventory and accounts receivable, it will have less cash available for growth, for reserve in emergencies, and for investment in profit-making opportunities. Exhibit 1–3 shows the flow of working capital and Exhibit 1–4 shows the time delays in this flow.

As we have seen, the goal of financial management is to maximize shareholder wealth subject to certain risk considerations. In this context we can look at the tradeoffs associated with the working capital flow decision. When we consider working capital flow decisions, we must include three factors: insolvency, profitability, and cost of funds.

1. *Insolvency*—Occurs when the company does not have sufficient cash or near-cash items to meet the demands of its creditors (accounts payable) and so defaults on its obligations and declares bankruptcy. The

smaller the level of cash and the slower the flow of funds, the higher the risk of insolvency.

2. *Profitability*—Also related to the amount of working capital and the speed of the flow of funds. For example, a high level of inventory allows a company to offer a wider range of goods for sale, which may lead to higher sales levels and larger profits. Conversely, a higher level of inventory could lead to lower profits if the goods can't be sold and the cost of carrying the inventory wipes out all of the company's profits.

3. *Cost of funds, or time value of money*—Related to the general level of interest rates in financial markets. When rates are high, it costs more to borrow money to finance inventory, which could lead to lower profits. Conversely, when rates are low, inventory financing may be quite cheap. Additionally, if rates are high, the return on marketable securities is very attractive vis-a-vis cash, and the increased investment income could increase profitability.

The relationship between risk and profitability is shown in Exhibit 1–5. In Panel A, we see that as the amount of liquidity increases, the risk of insolvency goes down. In Panel B, we see a curvilinear relationship between working capital levels and profitability. The manager's job is to balance these two factors of risk and profitability.

➤ PURPOSES OF CORPORATE CASH MANAGEMENT

There are four primary purposes of corporate cash management:

1. To have enough cash on hand to pay bills, payrolls, taxes, and all other obligations.
2. To have extra cash in reserve for greater-than-expected needs.
3. To minimize the amount of cash unnecessarily tied up in the business (primarily receivables and inventory).
4. To invest surplus cash in safe, profitable securities.

Because cash is part of working capital, effective cash management requires an understanding of the working capital policy of the firm. To understand fully the working capital policy, a cash manager must also understand the financial structure and goals of the firm. And, finally, the cash manager must relate these financial goals to the overall long-term corporate goals. Each level of financial management requires an understanding of the next higher level. While learning to do the best possible job in managing a corporation's day-to-day cash transactions, a cash manager will also be learning more about the company's total finances and objectives. Exhibit 1–6 shows the hierarchy that relates cash management to corporate goals.

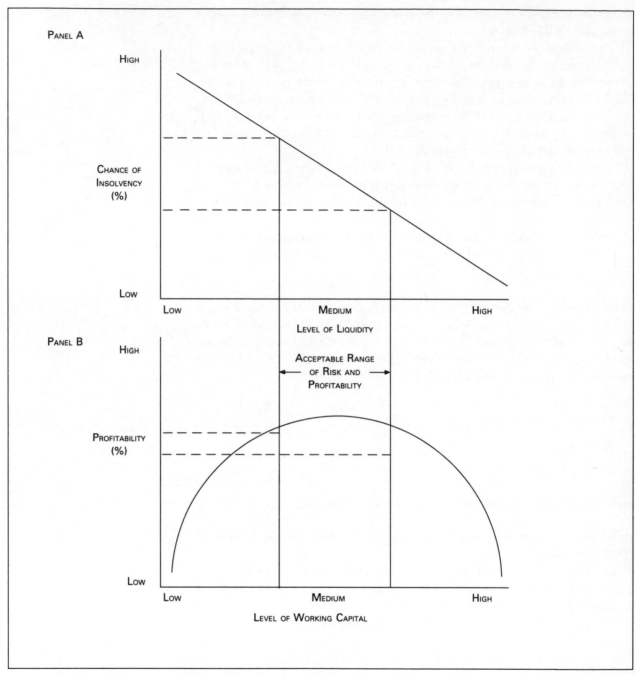

Exhibit 1–5   Risk, Profitability, and Working Capital

➤ Methods of Corporate Cash Management

Corporate cash management consists of several basic steps. The first step in cash management is cash forecasting, which enables a cash manager to predict a company's future need for cash by examining both past needs and future projections of sales, expenses, investments, and so on. The cash

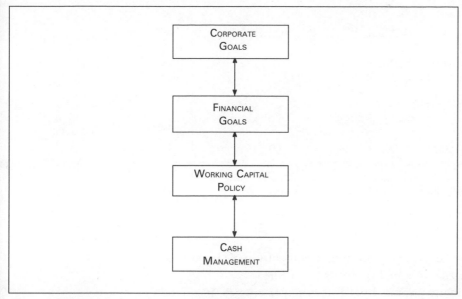

EXHIBIT 1–6   CASH MANAGEMENT AND CORPORATE GOALS

forecast is used to create a cash plan. A cash plan shows the amount of money the company will need to borrow during the year as well as the surplus cash that will be available for investment.

Cash mobilization involves several steps, which include freeing hidden cash, borrowing cash from banks and other lenders, and investing this extra cash more profitably. Cash mobilization techniques include faster billing, faster collection of receivables, and slower paying of bills. Banks can help in all these areas, so it is important to understand bank services, the charges for these services, and the best ways of maintaining good banking relations. Banks also help by lending money to companies, and finance companies provide money for receivables and inventories. Leasing can make additional cash available. Furthermore, companies often have surplus cash; it is important, therefore, to understand how to invest this surplus cash most effectively. Lastly, we discuss international cash management, which has its own special problems, including foreign exchange and slow, expensive communication.

➤ HIDDEN CASH

One of the most visible benefits of an effective cash management program is the cash it creates for other purposes. Cash often gets hidden in several predictable places within a company, including:

1. *Bank accounts.* Very often more cash than is necessary for day-to-day operations and emergency reserves is kept in demand deposits in banks.
2. *Accounts receivable.* Because of slow billing or a passive collection policy, a company may have more money than necessary tied up in accounts receivable.

Size of Company	Officer in Charge	Staff Size
Small	President/treasurer Vice-president/controller	0–2
Medium	Treasurer Assistant treasurer	1–10
Large	Assistant treasurer	10 or more

Exhibit 1–7   Organizational Structure for Cash Management in Companies of Various Sizes

3. *Inventory.* Because of poor inventory planning, a company may have much more money than necessary tied up in its inventory.
4. *Accounts payable.* If a company pays its bills faster than necessary, it is wasting cash that could be put to profitable uses elsewhere.

➤ ## Organizing for Corporate Cash Management

The way a company organizes to manage its cash depends primarily on the size of the company (see Exhibit 1–7). In a small company, officers may hold dual titles, such as president and treasurer, and there may be a very small staff or no staff responsible for cash management. In a medium-sized company, specialization begins to occur, and a staff is necessary for cash management. Large companies find it profitable to have a staff devoted exclusively to cash management and may even have individual cash managers in regional offices.

Exhibit 1–8 provides an overview of the treasury function for a large corporation, and Exhibit 1–9 shows the breakdown of this cash management function. Today's cash managers have day-to-day responsibilities, including bank relations, investments, short-term debt management, cash concentration, corporate finance planning and analysis, and cash disbursements. In addition, cash managers usually have some direct or indirect supervision over cash collection, accounts payable, and accounts receivable.

Given the many changes in recent years in cash management and the related complexities with the area, a new professional designation has been designed by the National Corporate Cash Management Association (NCCMA). The new designation is the CCM (Certified Cash Manager). Since 1986, more than 4,000 treasury professionals have taken a four-hour CCM exam covering specific cash management concepts. The NCCMA is currently planning a more comprehensive designation, the CTM (Certified Treasury Manager), which will cover most of the subjects illustrated in Exhibit 1–9 plus many of the other topics shown in Exhibit 1–8.

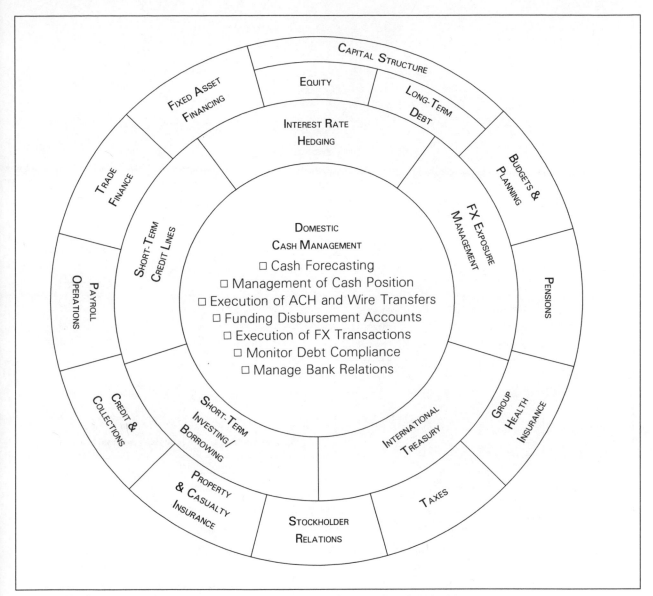

EXHIBIT 1–8 THE TREASURY FUNCTION FOR A LARGE CORPORATION. Source: *Reprinted with the permission of the NCCMA from* Essentials of Cash Management *by Ned C. Hill et al. © 1986.*

➤ SUMMARY

Corporate cash management is no longer an area in which a manager merely monitors checking accounts and bank balances. Today's cash manager needs to be up-to-date with current cash collection and disbursement techniques and must be able to implement cash concentration procedures.

Furthermore, advances in computer technology, electronic funds, and information transfers require the cash manager to be knowledgeable in both finance and computers and observant of changes in new products and developments in both fields.

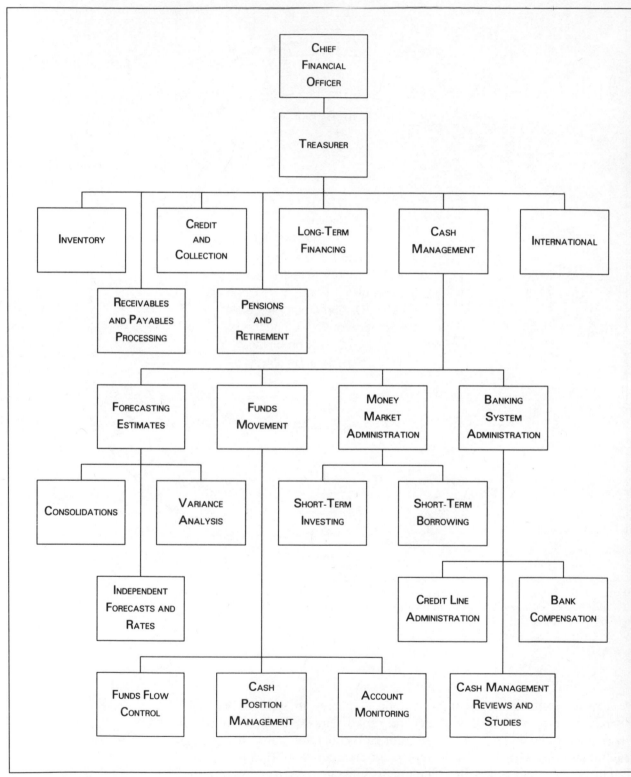

EXHIBIT 1–9   ORGANIZATION OF THE TREASURY FUNCTION.   Source: *Reprinted with the permission of the NCCMA from* Essentials of Management *by Ned. C. Hill et al.* © *1986.*

Chapter 2

The Corporation's Working Capital

By the end of this chapter, the reader will be able to:

1. Define the term *net working capital* in at least two ways.
2. Integrate working capital components.
3. Interpret liquidity ratios.
4. Differentiate between liquidity and liquidation.
5. Describe the basic characteristics of cash, marketable securities, accounts receivable, and inventories.

By "working capital" we mean the total of all those items shown on a company's balance sheet as short-term or current assets—that is, cash, marketable securities, accounts receivable, and inventories. Nevertheless, when we speak of working capital, we usually mean net working capital, which is current assets minus current liabilities (accounts payable, taxes and wages currently payable, short-term bank borrowing, and the current part of long-term debt). Net working capital is often considered a useful indication of the funds available to the company to finance its current operations. However, as we will see, net working capital is not synonymous with cash or liquidity.

➤ Components of Working Capital

In this chapter, we look closely at the four main components of working capital. We first show the relationship among these four components and briefly describe each. We then discuss each component in greater detail.

In Chapter 1, we showed that as a company operates, funds flow continuously from one asset to another. Exhibit 2–1 shows the short-term positions of this flow. Goods in inventory are sold to customers, thereby increasing accounts receivable. As customers pay their bills, the accounts receivable are

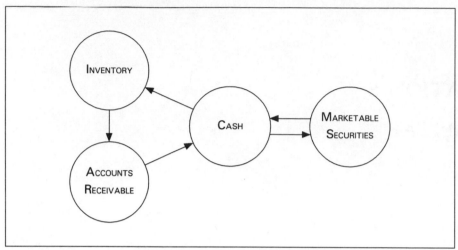

Exhibit 2–1   Cash Flow Cycle

turned into cash. If there is a surplus of cash, it may be used to purchase marketable securities. By holding marketable securities, a company can earn interest on its surplus money but can quickly convert these funds back into cash when necessary. The company then uses this cash to purchase additional goods for inventory, thus completing the cash flow cycle.

In a small company, the management of the cash flow cycle shown in Exhibit 2–1 is generally the responsibility of just one person. This single decision maker is still faced with the difficult problem of keeping the inflow of cash at a sufficient level to meet the expected and unexpected outflows, but, the coordination problems faced by a larger company are not present. Also, the evaluation of tradeoffs is not so complex because there is only one decision maker. In a large corporation, where a high degree of specialization is required to manage the cash flow cycles, the problem becomes much more complex. The cash, credit, marketing, purchasing, production, disbursement, and accounting management are all done by different individuals or departments. The lines of communication of most large organizations tend to be vertical (top to bottom) instead of horizontal. This makes the coordination of the cash flow cycle a quite complex management problem.

One way to view the cash flow cycle is by arranging the various activities that take place according to time. This time line will be used throughout this book to represent the sequencing of the inflows and outflows of cash through the company. Exhibit 2–2 shows a time line depicting the purchase by Company A and the sale by Company B of a product.

The number of individuals who are involved in the various events that take place during the cash flow cycle present an organizational problem which must be overcome for effective cash management. From the perspective of Company A (the buying company), placing the order is done by a purchasing agent, the receipt of goods is handled by a warehouse foreman, the receipt of the invoice is handled by the accounting or treasurer's office, the processing of the payment is done by both the accounting and treasurer's office, and the closing of the books is handled by the account-

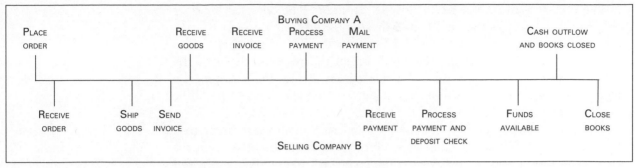

EXHIBIT 2–2 CASH FLOW TIME LINE

ing office. It is imperative that each of these individuals or departments be coordinated in their objectives and procedures in order to ensure that the company's profit and risk objectives are achieved. A similarly complex set of activities takes place in Company B.

Telling the cash flow manager to slow down outflows in order to conserve cash can have a negative impact on the relationship between the purchasing agent and the seller. Therefore, coordination is a must.

➤ THE NATURE OF CORPORATE CASH

When we speak of corporate cash balances, we are not speaking only of coins and notes. Business corporations do hold some cash in this sense, usually in the form of petty and till cash. But most corporate cash takes the form of demand deposits in commercial banks. Whether the deposits exist because the company has deposited cash or checks or because the bank has granted the company a short-term loan is unimportant here. Essentially, the corporate cash balance chiefly consists of the total demand deposits against which the company can write checks.

There are other current assets that we might call *near cash* or *cash equivalents*. These are marketable securities—*marketable* meaning that they can readily be converted into cash at any time without disrupting the normal routine of business operations. They are, therefore, almost as liquid as cash, so cash and marketable securities are often combined into a single category when making financial reports and analyzing working capital.

➤ REASONS FOR HOLDING CASH BALANCES

John Maynard Keynes identified three reasons for holding cash balances—the transactions motive, the precautionary motive, and the speculative motive—and almost every article or textbook on cash management repeats them. A fourth reason is that the pricing of most bank services and loans is based on a compensatory balance arrangement.

The transactions motive needs little explanation. The company must be able to pay its bills as they fall due. A large, positive amount of net working capital is no guarantee of being able to pay the bills. Cash must be on hand when the payments are due, and one of the responsibilities of the financial executive is to ensure that cash is available. (We discuss the techniques by which financial managers determine how much cash will be needed later in this book.)

The precautionary motive is closely related to the transactions motive. Precautionary cash holdings are necessary for transactions because no financial manager ever knows exactly what the company's transactions needs will be. If all future inflows and outflows of cash could be predicted with certainty, there would be no need for precautionary balances. Precautionary balances exist because of uncertainty, and the greater the uncertainty, the larger the precautionary balance must be. On the other hand, the need for precautionary cash is also a function of the ease with which outside, short-term funds can be obtained in a crisis; a company with excellent bank relations can usually rely on the bank to help it over a shortage of short-term cash and so can reduce its precautionary balances accordingly.

The speculative motive is not very relevant to most businesses. There are, however, some special situations in which a very unstable element in the company's operating environment offers a chance for speculative gain. One such element would be large and erratic price fluctuations of a raw material. The cocoa bean is one such material, and chocolate manufacturers sometimes buy very large consignments of cocoa if they believe the price to be unusually low. Stockpiling cash for acquisitions is another possibility but not a very likely one: The cash balances required would be very large, and acquisitions made by means of cash rather than stock are usually financed by bank borrowing rather than from cash balances. Perhaps the most common speculation arises in international trade. A company doing business with an overseas country whose currency fluctuates in value relative to the dollar may accumulate cash to profit from this instability in the exchange rate. But even here the precautionary motive is likely to predominate over the speculative motive. Most companies are more interested in making sure they are not hurt by adverse changes in the exchange rate than they are in trying to profit from favorable changes. To protect themselves against an adverse change, firms trading in more than one currency will hedge by dealing in foreign currency exchange markets.

A final reason for holding cash balances is the requirement of most commercial banks that customers hold compensating balances for loans or other services that they may be using. As most commercial banks unbundle their services and start pricing their loans and services on a fee basis, the role of compensating balances will diminish. However, this means of indirect payment seems to be a dominant reason why firms keep large balances of cash.

➤ THE COSTS OF
HOLDING CASH

Holding cash is a use of funds, not only in accounting convention but also in fact. By keeping an excess cash balance, a company ties up potential purchasing power. If the cash is in the form of demand deposits, it normally earns nothing and so is wholly unproductive. The exception is the NOW (negotiated order of withdrawal) account available only to individuals. This account pays interest while allowing checks to be drawn. If cash is invested in marketable securities, it earns interest. For example, short-term corporate certificates of deposit produced a yield of about 8 percent during 1991. But even this is probably far lower than the before-tax rate of return that the company earns on its operating assets. Thus, cash balances carry an opportunity cost. If cash is being held unnecessarily, the financial manager is not acting in the best interests of the stockholders.

Even if the company has exhausted the investment opportunities open to it, there is still no justification for holding large stocks of funds in the form of unproductive cash balances. The cash can be used to retire long-term debt, thereby reducing the corporate interest expense. Or it can be used to increase the wealth of the common shareholders, either by repurchasing some of the company's common stock to increase earnings per share on the rest or simply by issuing a cash dividend to the shareholders. (Using the latter option, however, may expose shareholders to an incremental income tax, which could substantially consume the dividend.)

There is another cost of holding cash. During the 1970s and 1980s, inflation became one of the major problems in the United States. It reached an annual rate of almost 20 percent. In this environment, funds tied up in idle cash balances are more than just unproductive—they are rapidly losing purchasing power. That is, there is a real cost, as well as an opportunity cost, to holding cash. In this type of inflationary environment, every effort must be made to keep idle cash balances at a minimum. The situation is analogous to running on a treadmill. As the speed of the treadmill increases, the jogger must run harder just to stay in place; so it is with high rates of inflation. The cash and marketable securities accounts must be managed more aggressively just to keep them from losing value. As we enter the 1990s, it appears that inflation will again rear its ugly head; strict cash management is a must if purchasing power is to be protected.

➢ THE COSTS OF
CASH INADEQUACY

Unfortunately, there are also costs associated with having insufficient cash. The ultimate cost of serious cash inadequacy is obviously illiquidity, which could lead to insolvency, followed by reorganization or liquidation. But even a less serious cash shortage has a cost. By a "less serious" cash shortage we mean one that is not a crisis but that makes the company slow to pay its bills.

This brings us to the other major cost of operating on inadequate cash balances: the danger of damaging the company's external relations—with its suppliers, its commercial bank or banks, other lenders, and the credit rating agencies. A company that constantly pays its bills late will eventually find itself asked to make all further purchases in cash, so an important source of short-term funds will have been lost. Similarly, a company that maintains very small balances in its demand deposits will be a very unprofitable customer for the banks, which may be unwilling to help if a real emergency arises. What's more, a chronic shortage of cash will lower the company's credit rating, as determined by Dun & Bradstreet and other rating agencies. Many financial intermediaries, such as insurance companies, base their lending decisions on these ratings, and therefore additional sources of funds will have been lost.

➤ INVESTING IN
MARKETABLE SECURITIES

We said earlier that a company's liquid funds can consist of both cash and cash equivalents. These cash equivalents are marketable securities, and unlike cash, they do earn some interest. One requirement of good asset management, then, is that the financial executive maintain as much of the company's liquid funds in this form as possible without endangering the company's ability to pay its bills on time.

The total cash balance maintained by companies covers both transaction requirements and precautionary requirements. It may be tempting to assume, then, that the financial executive must keep the transaction components in cash but can invest all the precautionary components in marketable securities. A little thought, however, will show that the issue is not so simple. Financial executives never know exactly what their company's transaction needs are going to be; if they did, they would not require any precautionary balances at all. So the decision about how much to invest is characterized by uncertainty.

Even without the element of uncertainty, however, a policy that set the desired level of marketable securities at a constant figure would not be realistic. The patterns of cash inflows and disbursements (payment of bills) fluctuate quite widely in most companies, so the corporate cash balances also fluctuate. A financial manager concerned about good asset management is more likely to find out how much cash should be kept in demand deposits and then to invest all surplus cash in interest-bearing securities than to keep a set amount in securities and allow demand deposits to fluctuate freely.

➤ SHORT-TERM
SECURITIES

Another aspect of sound asset management is the management of the investment portfolio to ensure that the company gets the best possible combination of return and protection of capital from its invested funds. A financial executive in a small company with limited funds may simply accept advice from the company's commercial bank or leave the task of portfolio management entirely to the bank. But when the sums to be invested are large, skilled investment in marketable securities can make a worthwhile contribution to shareholder wealth.

The only kind of security suitable for the investment of surplus cash is one that is readily marketable and has a short maturity. The funds may be a surplus at the moment but they will not be for very long. In two months, for example, the firm may find itself short of cash and have to liquidate its investment. Long-term government and corporate bonds are unsuitable because fluctuations in their value may more than offset any interest earned.

There are four criteria to consider when investing surplus cash. First, the investment must be sound, that is, largely free from any risk of default. Second, the maturity must be short enough to eliminate the risk of major price fluctuations. Third, a security must be readily marketable—that is, it should be possible to sell a reasonable volume of the security at short notice without forcing down its price. Fourth, all other characteristics being satisfactory, the financial executive should choose the investment with the highest possible yield; it would be unwise, however, to attempt to maximize yield at the expense of any of the other criteria.

➢ ACCOUNTS RECEIVABLE

Most cash managers exercise a great deal of control over the split between cash and marketable securities. But they have relatively little control over the level of accounts receivable. In fact, the company itself may have little control over accounts receivable because competitive conditions strongly affect the amount of credit the company must extend to its customers.

From the company's point of view, the best level of accounts receivable is that level that allows for the maximum amount of profit—that is, the mix of cash sales and credit sales that attracts the profitable customers without being excessively expensive. It is possible for certain organizations to sell for cash only, with no credit extended. Retailers can occasionally achieve this by not offering any credit or by offering a discount for cash payment. The use of credit cards also allows the participating merchant the opportunity for a credit sale if he or she is willing to pay the service fee of 3 to 7 percent of the sale.

Most companies, however, must offer credit. The two main elements to be considered are credit terms and collection policy. Setting the terms of payment involves deciding how much credit to grant each customer, how long customers have to pay, and whether to offer a discount for prompt payment. The collection policy of the company ensures that customers abide by the credit terms.

Credit is a marketing tool, and in some situations it is as important as price. As we have seen, a company is frequently unable to set its own credit terms because terms are decided by competition and by previous industry practice. However, if a company has unique products or if demand is very high for its products, the company may be able to offer less credit and still succeed. Similarly, some companies vary their credit policy depending on how busy they are. A company operating well below its capacity may offer substantial credit in order to increase sales. Another company, operating at its capacity, might tighten up its credit policies because it cannot handle any additional business.

Typical credit terms state when the bill is due and sometimes offer a discount for faster payment. For example, 2/10; net 30 means that customers may deduct 2 percent from the bill if they pay within 10 days; otherwise, the full amount is due in 30 days.

Suppose you purchase $100 worth of goods at these credit terms. The cash discount allows you to pay $98 instead of $100. If you do not take advantage of the discount, you are essentially getting a 20-day loan from the seller. However, for this loan you would pay $2/95 = 2.10 percent. By dividing 365/20 = 18.25, we get the number of 20-day periods at 2.10 percent per year. Thus 2.10 percent per period times 18.25 periods per year equals 38.4 percent per year, which is a 38.4 percent yearly cost on the original loan. In general, we can calculate the yearly cost of not taking a discount by the following formula:

$$\begin{matrix}\text{Yearly cost} \\ \text{of not taking} \\ \text{discounts}\end{matrix} = \frac{\text{Discount \%}}{\text{100-discount \%}} \times \frac{\text{Number of days in a year}}{\begin{matrix}\text{Number of days you have} \\ \text{use of the money}\end{matrix}}$$

Suppose that instead of paying at 30 days, as required by the terms of trade, you wait until the 50th day. This gives you an additional 20 days. What does this do to the cost of not taking the discount? Using the above formula:

$$\begin{matrix}\text{Yearly cost} \\ \text{of not taking} \\ \text{discounts}\end{matrix} = \frac{2}{100 - 2} \times \frac{365}{40} = 18.6\%$$

This reduction in the cost of not taking the discount from 38.4 percent down to 18.6 percent might make it attractive for the purchasers to delay paying their bills for as long as possible. This brings up the issue of collection policy.

Collection policy is the way in which a company makes sure that customers abide by the stated credit terms. The most important part of collecting bills is communication with the customer. First, whenever possible, the credit department should know the people in the customer company who are responsible for paying bills. This personal relationship will often help get the bill paid promptly; people do not like to let down a friend. Second, the company should promptly send out clear, error-free invoices. Third, if competitive conditions allow, the company should send statements of overdue bills at the end of 30 days. Finally, the company should age its accounts receivable, that is, show the dollar amount of bills outstanding for less than 30 days, 30 to 60 days, and so on. Then the company can compare the totals with similar figures for previous periods to determine if receivables are under control. In addition, aging pinpoints all overdue accounts that should be contacted personally to request payment.

If, after contacting the customer, the account payable remains unpaid, stronger collection actions may be necessary. One of the first steps is to insist on COD (cash on delivery) for any future purchases by the delin-

AVERAGE COLLECTION PERIOD	ANNUAL SALES		
	$6 MILLION	$60 MILLION	$600 MILLION
30 days	A/R = $500,000 Interest = $40,000	A/R = $5 million Interest = $400,000	A/R = $50 Million Interest = $4 million
60 days	A/R = $1 million Interest = $80,000	A/R = $10 million Interest = $800,000	A/R = $100 million Interest = $8 million
90 days	A/R = $1.5 million Interest = $120,000	A/R = $15 million Interest = $1.2 million	A/R = $150 million Interest = $12 million

Note: Interest on the accounts receivable is calculated at 8 percent.

EXHIBIT 2–3   HOW ACCOUNTS RECEIVABLE (A/R) VARY WITH SALES AND COLLECTION PERIODS

quent customer. Depending on the amount of money the customer owes, either legal action or use of a collection agency may be necessary. If the customer owes a large amount, the use of legal action may be justified. However, if the customer files for bankruptcy protection, the seller may receive little or nothing, while incurring legal expenses. Generally, for smaller amounts, the delinquent account can be sold to a collection agency, although this may also prove to be quite expensive, as most collection agencies take up to 50 percent of the amount recovered.

For many companies, accounts receivable constitute a large component of working capital. Why is the amount so large? Let's look at an example. If a company offers 30-day credit terms, then at any time it will have about 30 days of sales for which it has not been paid. Thirty days are 1/12 of a year; therefore, this company's accounts receivable will equal about 1/12 of its annual sales. If a company offers longer terms or has slow-paying customers or does not vigorously collect its bills, it may have 45 days worth of sales outstanding. Because 45 days is about 1/8 of a year, this company's accounts receivable will total about 1/8 of its annual sales. Clearly, large amounts of money can be tied up in accounts receivable. Furthermore, these two cases assume an even distribution of sales throughout the year. If there are strong seasonal fluctuations in sales, receivables could temporarily increase to an even larger fraction of annual sales. Exhibit 2–3 shows how accounts receivable and the interest on this money vary with sales and collection periods.

Thousands (or even millions) of dollars can be spent financing receivables. Why then do companies do it? Companies extend credit to customers primarily for marketing reasons. Customers are more willing to buy on credit, and very often a competitor is willing to offer credit. To make the sale, the company offers credit too. In most businesses, credit terms are determined by traditional industry practice and competing conditions.

In many companies, you will have to work closely with the marketing department in determining credit terms. It will then be your responsibility to have money available to finance accounts receivable. However, you do have some control over reducing the amount of funds tied up in receivables by billing and collecting quickly. (We discuss this in more detail in Chapter 5.) As a financial manager, your responsibilities concerning accounts receivable include maintaining the level of accounts at an affordable level and collecting the receivables as quickly as possible.

➢ Inventory

Inventories are the physical materials that a company either sells directly to its customers or uses to make its products. There are three main kinds of inventories:

1. Raw materials inventory, composed of materials used by a manufacturing company to make its products.
2. Work in process, or products as they are being manufactured.
3. Finished goods inventory, composed of the completed manufactured products or the purchased goods for a wholesale or retail company.

Companies maintain inventories for two principal reasons. It is more efficient and less expensive to buy from suppliers in large quantities. (Materials that cannot be used or sold immediately go into inventory.) Many customers demand a wide selection of products and fast delivery. If a company cannot offer its customers this wide choice and fast delivery, the company will lose sales to competitors. Although the annual cost of carrying inventory may be as much as 20 percent of the value of the inventory, companies must maintain it to remain competitive.

Costs of Inventory

Inventory often accounts for a large part of the working capital for many manufacturing, wholesale, and retail firms. However, these companies earn no direct return on their inventory. In fact, these companies must pay to maintain their inventories. Costs of maintaining inventories include storage space and facilities, handling within the warehouse, risk of theft or pilferage (cost of insurance), risk of deterioration, risk of obsolescence, and lost income on funds invested in inventory. These costs can add up to 20 percent or more of the inventory valuation per year. For example, an inventory valued at $10 million may cost $2 million per year to carry.

Reasons for Inventory

We must ask the same question about inventory that we ask about accounts receivable: Why is this expense necessary? Companies carry inventory so that they can quickly satisfy customers' needs and avoid losing customers to competitors. For example, if you run a record store and a customer comes in looking for Beethoven's Ninth Symphony, you must have it in stock if you want to make the sale. Furthermore, since the customer could have just as well been looking for Mozart, Ravel, or Stravinsky, you must have their works in stock, too. And, of course, you will need more than one copy of each. The next three customers who come in may all want Beethoven; unless your inventory can handle these requests, you will lose the sales.

In a manufacturing company, the need for inventory arises for different reasons. Most manufacturing processes create products at a regular rate, say one unit every minute. However, the demand for these products is not even. One day, the factory may have orders for 200 units and the next day have orders for 1,000 units. Inventory acts as a buffer between these different rates of supply and demand.

Companies require raw materials inventory for a similar reason. A company may use a certain raw material at a rate of one pound per hour. The raw material supplier could conceivably deliver that one pound every hour, but it would be more efficient to make a single eight-pound delivery each day. It may be even more efficient to make a larger delivery once a week or once a month. Buying in larger quantities is more efficient and usually cheaper. Again, inventory acts as a buffer between supply and demand.

A financial manager's principal problem with inventory, as with the other components of working capital, is determining the optimum levels. If your company has too little inventory, it may lose sales because it does not have products to sell, or it may have to stop manufacturing temporarily because it lacks raw materials. On the other hand, if inventory levels are allowed to rise unnecessarily, a company will have money tied up in unnecessary materials. In addition, the company will have the extra costs of storage, handling, and insurance, as well as the risk of obsolescence.

DETERMINING INVENTORY LEVELS

A new alternative to holding inventory is a system introduced by the Japanese called Just-In-Time (JIT) Inventory. In this system, the level of inventory is reduced to a minimum level (zero). The JIT system uses flexible production, small lot sizes, and high-quality output to produce goods only as they are needed. Hence, JIT systems can be used to reduce raw material inventory, work in process, and also finished goods inventory.

Exhibit 2–4 summarizes the components of working capital, the form of these components, and the problems that will arise if any component is too large or too small.

➤ WORKING CAPITAL AND CASH

Although cash is a part of working capital and working capital is closely connected with cash needs, *working capital is not the same thing as cash*. Indeed, a company may have millions of dollars of working capital and yet be seriously short of cash. Our first task is to make this difference clear and show how it arises. Then, in Chapter 3, we will look at the problems of managing cash flows.

We begin by looking at the current part of a company's balance sheet. In Exhibit 2–5, using the definitions given previously, we can say that

COMPONENT	FORMS	PROBLEMS IF COMPONENT IS TOO SMALL	PROBLEMS IF COMPONENT IS TOO LARGE
Cash	Demand deposits in banks	Risk of running out of cash; insolvency	Loss of interest from investing surplus funds
Marketable securities	Treasury bills Certificates of deposit Commercial paper	Insufficient safety margin for cash account	No problem other than investing in an optimal mix of securities
Accounts receivable	Outstanding invoices to customers	May indicate over-cautious credit policy Noncompetitive credit policy Business downturn	May indicate over-generous credit policy Possible collection problems Money tied up without a direct return
Inventory	Raw materials Work in process Finished goods	Inability to deliver customers' orders quickly	Money tied up without a direct return Additional costs of storage, insurance, and handling Risk of obsolescence

EXHIBIT 2–4   COMPONENTS OF WORKING CAPITAL

Truetool has working capital of $2.5 million and net working capital of $1.0 million. But does it have *adequate* working capital? And how do we judge the adequacy of working capital?

➤ RATIO ANALYSIS

One way to judge the adequacy of working capital is to use ratio analysis. Two ratios are most relevant to the management of working capital. The first of these, the *current ratio*, is computed by dividing current assets by current liabilities. For Truetool, the result is as follows:

$$\frac{\text{Current assets}}{\text{Current liabilities}} = \frac{\$2,500,000}{\$1,500,000} = 1.67$$

But what does this mean? We need to have some kind of standard of comparison. If the average current ratio in the tool industry is 2.5, we can say that Truetool's current ratio is below average. But even if a company's current ratio is different from the industry average, we can-

CURRENT ASSETS	
Cash	$ 500,000
Marketable securities	300,000
Accounts receivable	800,000
Inventory	900,000
Total current assets	$2,500,000
CURRENT LIABILITIES	
Accounts payable	$ 700,000
Accrued wages	300,000
Notes payable	500,000
Total current liabilities	$1,500,000

EXHIBIT 2–5   TRUETOOL, INC. — PARTIAL BALANCE SHEET AS OF DECEMBER 31, 1989

not immediately say that the firm is in trouble. In our example, the current ratio of Truetool is below the industry norm. This could indicate that Truetool's managers are very efficient in handling current assets, economizing on the amount of funds tied up in short-term accounts. The funds they free up may be used for projects that will increase profits. On the other hand, this example could indicate that Truetool does not have enough current assets to effectively compete in the proper markets, because of either restrictive credit policies or lack of a full line of inventory. Similarly differing interpretations can be made for individual current ratios that are above industry norms. The only thing we can say for certain at this point is that, when an individual ratio differs from the norm, it should be a warning signal. It may be a good sign or a bad one, depending on further analysis.

The other relevant ratio is the *quick ratio*, sometimes called the *acid-test ratio*. It differs from the current ratio in that it considers only those current assets that can readily be converted into cash. (For example, inventory is excluded from the quick ratio because it usually cannot be converted into cash whenever one wishes—except, perhaps, by selling it at scrap prices.) The quick ratio is computed by dividing quick assets—cash, securities, and accounts receivable—by total current liabilities. For Truetool, the result is as follows:

$$\frac{\text{Quick assets}}{\text{Current liabilities}} = \frac{\$1,600,000}{\$1,500,000} = 1.07$$

The quick ratio is more useful than the current ratio because it tells us something even if we have no industry standard to compare it with. We know that if Truetool could immediately collect its accounts receivable and sell its securities at the value at which they are carried on its books, its cash balance would exceed its outstanding current liabilities, though not by much. Does this mean that Truetool's working capital is adequate?

Period Outstanding	Dollar Amount of A/R	Percent of Total
0–30 days	$400,000	50%
30–60 days	325,000	41
60–90 days	50,000	6
Over 90 days	25,000	3
Total	$800,000	100%

Exhibit 2–6   Truetool's Accounts Receivable Aging Schedule

➤ The Question
of Timing

We still cannot say whether or not Truetool has adequate working capital because our analysis to this point has left out one vital element: *timing*. We will now rephrase our question; instead of asking whether Truetool has adequate working capital, we will ask, "Is Truetool going to be able to pay all its bills as they fall due?" The answer is that we still do not know. It depends on when the bills fall due and how long it will take to collect the accounts receivable.

To get some indication of when a company can expect to receive the cash flow from the collection of its accounts receivable, we can look at its average collection period and its accounts receivable aging schedule. The average collection period, in days, can be calculated by dividing accounts receivable by sales per day. Let's assume that Truetool's 1989 sales amounted to $9,733,333. In that case, its average collection period would be as follows:

$$\frac{\text{Accounts receivable}}{\text{Sales per day}} = \frac{\$800,000}{(\$9,733,333 \div 365)} = 30 \text{ days}$$

The average collection period tells us how long it will take, on the average, to collect accounts receivable from the day of sale. In general, the longer the average collection period, the less stringent the firm's credit policy.

A more detailed statement of the volume and percentage of the accounts receivable that have been outstanding for various lengths of time is contained in the aging of accounts receivable schedule. Exhibit 2–6 shows Truetool's aging schedule.

If we make a couple of simple assumptions, we can see just why timing is important. Assume, therefore, that all of Truetool's accounts payable are for materials bought on terms of net 30 days and that the average maturity of the accounts payable is half this amount of time, or 15 days. Assume, too, that Truetool's terms of sale to its customers are net 30 days. We have already established that the average collection period is 30 days.

What does this imply about Truetool's cash requirements in the coming month? Assuming that the company's business is stable—that is, that sales are neither expanding nor shrinking — we can assume that during the next 30 days the company will have to pay all its accounts payable, that is, $700,000. But it will have collected only about half its receivables, or about $400,000. This leaves a net deficit of $300,000. If we further assume that the $300,000 of accrued wages must also be paid during this period, this gives us a net outflow of $600,000. Cash alone will not be adequate to meet these net outflows. The company will have to sell its marketable securities, and even then it will be left dangerously short of cash, especially if the $500,000 note soon becomes payable. Thus, a company that at first sight seemed to have adequate working capital now appears to be heading for insolvency because it is ignoring the timing of its cash flows.

➤ THE CASH FLOW CYCLE
AND THE TIME LINE

The time it takes for cash to flow through the working capital accounts and return to cash is a measurable quantity of time called the cash flow cycle. Essentially, the cycle begins when the organization pays cash for investments in current assets and ends when cash flows back to the company as payment for goods or services sold in the marketplace. To be more specific, the cash flow cycle equals the average age of current assets or inventory plus the average age of accounts receivable minus the average age of accounts payable.

The cash flow cycle can be defined as :

$$
\begin{aligned}
\text{Cash flow cycle} \ = \ & \text{Average age of inventory + Average} \\
& \text{age of accounts receivable – Average} \\
& \text{age of accounts payable} \\[8pt]
= \ & \text{Number of days in the planning period} \\[6pt]
& \times \left(\frac{\text{Average inventory}}{\text{Cash operating expenses}} \right. \\[6pt]
& + \frac{\text{Average age of accounts receivable}}{\text{Sales}} \\[6pt]
& \left. - \frac{\text{Average age of accounts payable}}{\text{Cost of goods sold}} \right)
\end{aligned}
$$

One important part of the corporate cash manager's job is to control the amount of time each of the working capital accounts is using. In our discussion so far we've seen how average inventory can be divided into various subelements by use of the cash flow time line. Referring back to Exhibit 2–2, we can see the various steps taken by the purchasing company in order to get the material purchased into inventory and the accounting information flow that relates to payment for the goods. Additionally in our discussion of inventory, we saw how holding various levels of goods and material would lead to different levels of expense. Putting both of these discussions together in the form of a time line will allow us to see how the various steps taken to handle and pay for inventory are related to cash flow. In Exhibit 2–7 we combine the inventory concept with the cash flow time line.

Looking at Exhibit 2–7 we see that the time period when the inventory is in physical possession of the company will determine how much we have to spend to handle the inventory; this is a cash outflow. Such techniques as JIT inventory will reduce this time period and reduce some of the handling costs thereby reducing a cash outflow. However it must be remembered that JIT has other costs (outflows) associated with its implementation; these must be considered. The paying for inventory and the receipt of the proceeds from the sale of the goods is another portion of the cash flow cycle that needs to be considered by the cash manager. Anything the corporate cash manager can do to speed up the inflows and slow down the outflows will contribute to the more efficient management of the company. The remainder of this book is devoted to forecasting, planning, and budgeting the physical, information, and cash flows as depicted in Exhibit 2–7. As we shall see from the perspective of the entire company, this can be quite a complex process.

➢ An Integrative Approach
To Working Capital Management

It should now be clear that an increase in net working capital does not necessarily translate into an increase in liquidity. One reason for this is that increases in net working capital often result from increases in operating assets, not of increases in operating liabilities. These operating assets, such as accounts receivable or inventory, are usually tied up in operations and are not commonly liquidated (prematurely) to pay bills. Bills are typically paid with liquid financial assets, such as cash and marketable securities. Thus, only the liquid financial assets can be useful in assessing a firm's liquidity. Furthermore, corporate insolvency usually results when the firm fails to service debt obligations or callable liabilities in a timely manner. Consequently, a good measure of corporate liquidity can be calculated by taking the difference between liquid financial assets and callable liabilities. This is referred to as the *net liquid balance*.

Exhibit 2–8 shows how the net liquid balance is actually a part of net working capital. *Net working capital* is easily calculated as either the difference between current assets and current liabilities (as described earlier) or the difference between long-term liabilities/equities and long-term assets (such as fixed assets). The former definition is often misinterpreted as the difference between two liquid components, whereas the latter definition suggests that the residual of long-term liabilities over long-term assets is used to finance current assets, some of which may be liquid. The latter definition also enables us to analyze the current assets and liabilities as consisting of both liquid financial/callable components and operating components.

Net working capital is actually the summation of working capital requirements (current operating assets minus current operating liabilities) and the net liquid balance. This suggests that only a part of net working capital is liquid. Clearly, as a firm grows, current operating assets will increase. If current operating liabilities do not increase at the same rate as

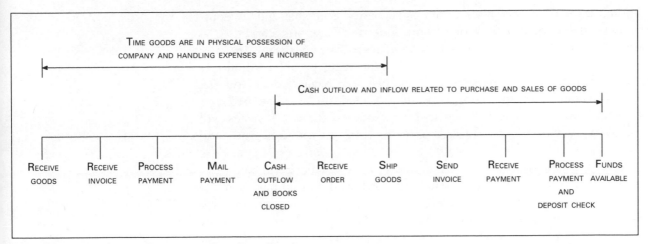

EXHIBIT 2–7   TRUETOOL'S INVENTORY AND CASH FLOW TIME LINE

current operating assets (which is true when the firm pays its suppliers before it receives payment from customers), then the firm will find that its net liquid balance will decrease (assuming the firm does not increase its long-term funding arrangements). This may be true even though the firm is generating accounting profits. As long as the increase in working capital requirements exceeds the increase in profits (profits are included in the long-term liabilities/equities part of Exhibit 2–8 due to increases in stockholders' equity), the firm will find itself reducing its liquidity levels. This highlights one of the fundamental weaknesses of the traditional liquidity ratios, such as the current ratio or quick ratio. These ratios include both liquid financial assets and operating assets in their formulas. Since operating assets are tied up in operations, including these assets in a liquidity ratio is not very useful from an ongoing concern perspective. Note the difference between a liquidity perspective and a liquidation perspective. A *liquidation perspective* assumes that in the event of a crisis, assets may be sold off to meet financial obligations, whereas a *liquidity perspective* assumes that the firm's financial obligations are met without impairing the viability of future operations. From an ongoing perspective, a new ratio—net liquid balance to total assets—may be more indicative of liquidity than either the current ratio or the quick ratio.

➢ CASH FLOWS AND FUNDING NEEDS

The management of working capital involves more than just monitoring liquidity balances. It also includes managing accounts receivable and inventories as well as acquiring appropriate levels of financing from suppliers and creditors. To forecast the amount and timing of its funding requirements, management usually needs to develop a detailed cash forecast. The cash forecast, which we will discuss in later chapters, is also useful in determining the appropriate maturity of funding sources.

Some level of current assets, such as accounts receivable and inventories, will always be required for corporate needs. These are referred to as permanent levels of current assets (or permanent current assets). In addition, some level of current liabilities, such as accounts payable, will always be on hand. If the firm pays its suppliers before it receives payment, the firm will generally be in a borrowing situation due to its permanent layers of current assets. As we will see in later chapters, the firm's needs will increase even more during stages of growth. How fast the firm grows and how easily it can obtain funding from institutional sources will affect the amounts and types of funds it should pursue. For example, permanent layers of accounts receivable and inventories should be financed by long-term sources if management is concerned about exposure to refinancing risk (that is, rising interest rates or the possibility of funding becoming unavailable). This is consistent with the matching principle, which states that long-term or permanent assets should be financed by long-term or permanent sources, and short-term assets should be financed by short-term sources. This concept is depicted in Exhibit 2–9. However, management may choose not to be conservative and decide to finance permanent needs with short-term debt because it believes that short-term debt is generally less expensive than long-term debt. This would be considered an aggressive management approach because the firm would be subject to the risk of rising interest rates and to problems with refinancing retiring debt. Nevertheless, some studies suggest that management quite often attempts to minimize short-term interest rates despite increasing financing risks.

➤ Working Capital Strategies

Most firms experience seasonal or cyclical fluctuations in their operations. For example, construction firms typically experience operating peaks in the spring and summer, whereas retailers experience peak operations around Christmas. Similarly, corporations increase their working capital levels when sales are strong and then reduce their levels of inventories and receivables when the economy weakens. These seasonal buildups (or reductions) in current assets accounts are classified as temporary or fluctuating current assets. However, the firm's current assets rarely decline to zero. As a result, the firm will maintain some level of permanent current assets. The manner in which the firm's temporary and permanent current asset requirements are financed is defined as the firm's working capital strategy.

In general, the firm should employ a matching strategy, which attempts to match asset and liability maturities. Under this strategy, the firm's fixed assets and permanent working capital are financed with long-term sources of funds, whereas the firm's temporary current assets are financed with short-term sources of funds. However, in practice, uncertainty about the lives of assets makes exact maturity matching impossible. Even if the dollar amounts of permanent and temporary current assets could be precisely determined, the exact timing of asset liquidation is difficult to forecast. We

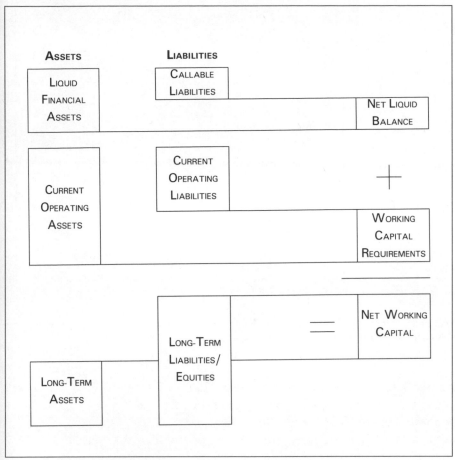

Assets   **Liabilities**

Liquid Financial Assets

Callable Liabilities

Net Liquid Balance

Current Operating Assets

Current Operating Liabilities

$+$

Working Capital Requirements

Long-Term Liabilities/ Equities

$-$

Net Working Capital

Long-Term Assets

Exhibit 2–8   Integrative Approach to Working Capital Management. Source: *Joel Shulman and Ismael Dambolena, "Analyzing Corporate Solvency,"* Journal of Cash Management *6 (September/October 1986) 35–38. Reprinted by permission.*

may also have difficulty forecasting the amount of short-term and long-term financing that will be available at a given time.

On the other hand, companies sometimes use short-term funds to finance a portion of the firm's permanent current assets. Many small companies do not have access to the long-term capital markets, and are forced to rely heavily on short-term bank and trade credit. In addition, even some large businesses have been forced to operate with short-term funds during periodic credit squeezes. Financing permanent needs with short-term sources of funds is known as an aggressive strategy. The risk associated with this strategy is that the firm might not be able to refinance the short-term debt when the funds come due or that interest rates might increase significantly overnight. As a rule, however, the interest rate on short-term funds is lower than that on long-term funds. Therefore, financial executives may attempt to finance as much of their permanent current asset needs as possible with short-term debt, hoping to minimize their interest burden.

To protect against the danger of being unable to obtain adequate short-term financing during periods of "tight" money, financial executives may

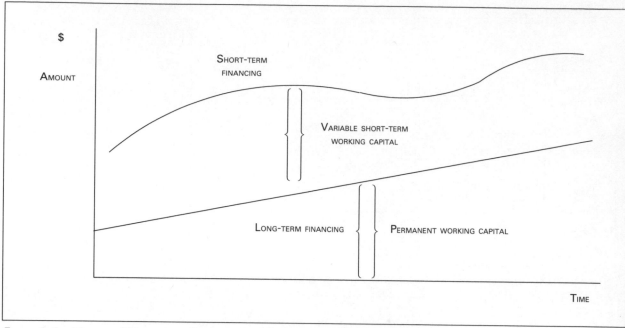

Exhibit 2–9   Matching Maturities of Financing Sources and Working Capital Assets

rely on long-term financing to cover some short-term needs. Under this approach, which is termed a conservative working capital strategy, the firm uses long-term capital to finance fixed assets, permanent current assets, and a portion of temporary current assets. By using long-term sources of capital to finance short-term needs, the firm virtually assures itself of having adequate capital. However, as we noted, the cost of long-term financing is generally higher than that of short-term financing. Thus, under the conservative strategy, the firm reduces its risk of being unable to obtain financing but typically pays a higher interest rate.

➢ Summary

Working capital is often misinterpreted as being synonymous with firm liquidity. In fact, only a part of net working capital is liquid; the balance of net working capital is tied up in firm operations. Liquidity is largely a function of a firm's growth and the timing of receipts and payments. In situations where payments are made to suppliers before customers pay, growth in sales generally results in lower liquidity.

Preparing a cash flow forecast assists managers in assessing the timing and maturity of funding needs. With a cash forecast, management can determine more easily the type of funding to procure and the firm's ability to grow with available funds. In the chapters that follow, we will describe cash forecasts and discuss planning strategies.

Chapter 3

Planning Cash Flow

By the end of this chapter, the reader will be able to:

LEARNING OBJECTIVES

1. Calculate cash flow from operations in two ways.
2. Describe free cash flow.
3. Describe the new FASB "Statement of Cash Flows" in general terms.
4. Prepare and interpret a cash flow statement.

As the operations of a company go on day by day and month by month, they cause cash to be received and cash to be disbursed. Moreover, these receipts and disbursements will not always balance out to a steady, gradual increase in the company's cash, even if the company is making steady profits. Large cash outflows will occur at times, such as when income taxes are due or a major new capital investment must be paid for. Unusually large inflows may also occur, such as when a major item of contract work is paid for by the customer. Thus, over the short term, the cash balances of any company fluctuate considerably.

There are two reasons for planning cash flow. The first reason is to ensure that short-term sources of funds can be negotiated and arranged well in advance of having to use them. As the cash flows fluctuate, there may be a time when cash balances fall below zero. These shortfalls must be anticipated so that the liquidity of the firm is not jeopardized. It is much easier to negotiate a short-term loan in advance (thereby giving the indication of good management) than it is to attempt to secure funds at the last moment in a crisis.

The second reason for planning cash flow is just as important as the first, especially during periods of high inflation. As a result of fluctuations, cash balances may be much higher than immediate needs. This idle cash must be invested in short-term money-market instruments as soon as the cash becomes available so as to preserve its purchasing power and contribute to the firm's profitability. Whether the firm's cash budget indicates a shortfall or a surplus, the management of the firm must take the appropriate action in a timely manner.

➤ Planning Cash Flow
and Planning Profits

Although there is a relationship between them, cash flows are not the same as profit. Profit is an accounting concept designed to measure the overall performance of the company. It is a somewhat nebulous concept, open to various measurement techniques and accounting conventions, each of which produces somewhat different results, which are then open to different interpretations.

In contrast, cash flows are not a measure of a company's performance. Take two opposite extremes: a young, profitable company sinking as many funds as it can get into a new venture and an old, unprofitable company heading for bankruptcy. The results in terms of cash flow are likely to be the same: declining cash balances. A company can show a handsome profit and a net cash outflow in the same month if it chooses to pay for new capital equipment in that month. It can equally well show a substantial loss and an increased cash balance in one month if the results of new financing or the proceeds from the sale of substantial fixed assets are received in that month.

Moreover, the concept of cash is not nebulous. Either the company has a certain amount of cash or it has not. And a lack of cash is critical. A company can sustain losses for a time without suffering permanent damage, but a company that has no cash is insolvent and in imminent danger of bankruptcy no matter what its profit picture may be.

Thus, many financial transactions that do not enter into the calculation of profit—such as buying new fixed assets, getting additional financing, and paying dividends—enter into cash flows. Similarly, some transactions that enter into the determination of profit—notably, the deduction of depreciation and amortization expenses—do not enter into cash flows because they are noncash transactions with no effect on cash balances.

➤ Planning Periods

Cash flow planning consists of both short- and long-term forecasts. The principal purpose of a short-term forecast is to identify *temporary* cash shortages or surpluses and to deal with them. Once the corporation's long-term goals and objectives have been established, the forecast is used to plan how to achieve the desired target.

Generally, the short-term cash flow forecast is linked to a longer-term forecast. Many firms prepare a long-term forecast of one to five years that includes long-term expansion, growth expectations, long-term financing, and capital investment concerns. After developing a long-term forecast, the firm's financial managers prepare a short-term forecast of one month to one year that is consistent with the overall plan. Obviously, a long-term forecast of one to five years is subject to errors based on unanticipated events. The long-term forecast, however, does provide goals for management to strive for and can be updated as new information becomes available.

Short-term forecasts are often prepared on a receipts minus disbursements basis, whereas longer-term forecasts are usually based on an

Cash at start of month	$30,000
CASH INFLOWS	
Accounts receivable collections	$55,000
Royalty payment	25,000
Proceeds of sale of surplus fixed assets	15,000
Total cash inflows	$95,000
CASH OUTFLOWS	
Salaries and wages (net)	$24,000
Raw material purchases	19,500
Supplies	5,000
Miscellaneous expenses	10,000
Rent	4,000
Income tax payment	25,000
Payroll taxes	7,500
Total cash outflows	$95,000
Cash at end of month	$30,000

EXHIBIT 3–1   CASH FLOW PLAN FOR ONE MONTH

adjusted-net-income approach (also described as an indirect approach, which we will discuss later). The short-term forecast is focused on the timing of cash flows and on the availability of cash to meet bills as they come due. An insufficient level of cash on hand could cause the firm to pass up valuable trade discounts and, at the extreme, could cause the firm to file for bankruptcy. Thus, the short-term forecast concentrates on the actual receipt and disbursement of cash.

Since cash flow planning is concerned with fluctuations in cash balances, the interval of time used for planning is a more important consideration than the length of the whole planning period. The most common interval is one month. That is, a financial manager forecasts cash inflows and outflows over one month and then calculates beginning- and end-of-month balances. This procedure is repeated for the other eleven months of the year if the overall planning horizon is one year. Using one month as the time period has the advantage of coinciding with the accounting period of most companies and probably also with their official period for collecting receivables.

But many companies use a shorter interval of time, and some large companies forecast by the day. Why such a short interval? If the company forecasts by the month and shows adequate balances at the end of each month, isn't it a waste of time to use a shorter interval? That this is not true is dramatically shown by Exhibits 3–1 and 3–2. Suppose a company uses a planning interval of one month. Its cash flow plan for one month might look like that in Exhibit 3–1.

	Week 1	Week 2	Week 3	Week 4
Cash at start of week	$30,000	($ 2,250)	($ 9,500)	($ 2,250)
Cash Inflows				
Accounts receivable collections	$12,000	$15,000	$11,000	$17,000
Royalty payment				25,000
Proceeds of sale of surplus fixed assets			10,000	5,000
Total cash inflows	$12,000	$15,000	$21,000	$47,000
Cash Outflows				
Salaries and wages (net)	$ 6,000	$ 6,000	$ 6,000	$ 6,000
Raw material purchases	5,500	5,000	4,000	5,000
Supplies	1,250	1,250	1,250	1,250
Miscellaneous expenses	2,500	2,500	2,500	2,500
Rent	4,000			
Income tax payment	25,000			
Payroll taxes		7,500		
Total cash outflows	$44,250	$22,250	$13,750	$14,750
Cash at end of week	($ 2,250)	($ 9,500)	($ 2,250)	$30,000

Exhibit 3–2   The Same Cash Flow Plan Broken Down by the Week

It appears from Exhibit 3–1 that all is well. The company's cash balance will stay steady at $30,000. But will it? Suppose we break down this forecast by the week, as is done in Exhibit 3–2.

As can be seen from Exhibit 3–2, although the monthly cash flow forecast looks fine, the weekly forecast shows that the company will be in considerable trouble before the first week is over. Such a company would do well to choose a planning period not longer than one week and possibly shorter.

Other factors affecting the choice of a planning interval are:

☐ Inflation rates and opportunity costs.
☐ Size of cash flows.
☐ Executive time available for cash flow planning and cash management.
☐ Predictability of the size of inflows and outflows.
☐ Predictability of the timing of inflows and outflows.
☐ Size of cash balances.

Inflation Rates and Opportunity Cost

When inflation rates are at record-high levels, the necessity for actively managing the firm's cash position is obvious. Not only is it very expensive to borrow short-term funds, but also there may be periods when no funds are available at any price. A corporation that has not secured a commitment in advance will be unable to meet its cash requirements. Excess cash must be invested as soon as it becomes available so as to avoid the erosion in purchasing power. Making a cash budget also allows the financial manager to see the impact of various decisions on speeding up or slowing down cash flows.

Companies that plan their cash by the day usually have very large cash flows over short intervals. For example, $1 million invested at 12 percent for one day yields $328.75—a sum that makes it well worth one person's time to plan and invest cash daily. In contrast, $10,000 at 12 percent for one day yields less than $3.28. Thus, a company whose cash balances day to day do not fluctuate much more than this could hardly justify the management time required for daily cash planning.

SIZE OF CASH FLOWS

Executive time is one of the scarcest resources of most companies. Thus, it may be that even if the time spent on daily cash flow planning would earn a return greater than the salary of the person who does it, that person's time might still be spent more productively in doing other work. Such a situation dictates a longer planning interval.

EXECUTIVE TIME

Usually, the size of cash inflows and outflows is much more predictable than their timing. But when it is not, unexpectedly small inflows combined with unexpectedly large outflows could create a serious cash shortage over a short time. This possibility must be avoided, either by carrying large balances to provide a safety margin or by maintaining a very short planning interval and a continuous watch on how actual events are conforming to plan. Which alternative is adopted will depend on the size of the balances needed and the management time available for short-interval cash planning.

PREDICTABILITY OF THE SIZE OF CASH FLOWS

It is often impossible to predict with accuracy the timing of cash flows, particularly cash inflows. For example, if cash inflows are received through the mail, they may arrive a day earlier or a day later than expected. Usually, because it cannot be known exactly when a customer will mail a check, the timing is much more uncertain than this. It may vary by several days or even by several weeks. Under these circumstances, daily cash flow plans are subject to error and may be no more useful than weekly or monthly forecasts.

PREDICTABILITY OF THE TIMING OF CASH FLOWS

From the point of view of avoiding insolvency, the size of cash balances in relation to cash flow has a bearing on the planning interval. If cash balances are large, temporary variations within a long planning interval such as a month are unlikely to place them in jeopardy. But if the company is operating on inadequate balances, a strong net cash outflow over only a few days may bring balances down to dangerously low levels. In such circumstances, a short planning interval is necessary for survival, even if it could not be economically justified on any other grounds. For this reason, a company that normally uses a planning interval of one month may switch to weekly planning when its cash balances are dangerously low.

SIZE OF CASH BALANCES

➢ DEVELOPING THE PLAN

Once the planning horizon and planning interval have been determined, the actual planning can begin. The first step is to forecast expected cash

	JANUARY	FEBRUARY	MARCH	APRIL	MAY	JUNE
Cash at start of month	$19,680	($10,020)	($ 1,820)	$13,180	$22,230	$13,670
CASH INFLOWS						
Sales receipts	$55,000	$57,000	$69,000	$61,000	$64,000	$65,000
Insurance claim					7,000	
Royalties on patent	4,000			3,500		
Total cash inflows	$59,000	$57,000	$69,000	$64,500	$71,000	$65,000
CASH OUTFLOWS						
Labor payroll	$23,000	$23,500	$24,000	$24,500	$31,000	$25,200
Salaries	4,800	4,800	4,800	5,600	5,600	5,600
Raw materials payments	31,000	15,500	18,250	11,650	28,760	15,625
Payments for supplies	2,400	1,800	2,000	2,000	2,000	2,000
Insurance			750			
Lease payments	1,000	1,000	1,500	1,000	1,000	1,500
Marketing expenses	500	500	1,500	500	500	500
Miscellaneous expenses	1,000	1,200	1,200	1,200	1,200	1,200
Dividends	18,000					
Income taxes	7,000			9,000		
Professional fees		500			4,000	
New production equipment					5,500	
Total cash outflows	$88,700	$48,800	$54,000	$55,450	$79,560	$51,625
Cash at end of month	($10,020)	($ 1,820)	$13,180	$22,230	$13,670	$27,045

EXHIBIT 3–3   SIX-MONTH CASH FLOW FORECAST BY MONTH

receipts during each planning interval. Sales receipts are normally based on the sales forecast and experience of the pattern of receivables collections. Other receipts, such as those from the sale of fixed assets, royalty incomes, and investment income, can also be predicted with a fair degree of accuracy. Later in this chapter we will discuss a technique that helps when receipts are more uncertain. Meanwhile, it is sufficient to note that where there is doubt about the size or timing of receipts, the planner should forecast conservatively. Receipts higher than the forecasts may result in cash that might otherwise have been invested profitably, but receipts lower than expected may expose the company to illiquidity, which is far more serious.

Exhibit 3–3 is an example of a six-month cash flow forecast done by the month. The upper part of the exhibit, "Cash Inflows," illustrates this first step of planning cash flow.

The next step is to forecast cash disbursements. Here planners again lean on experience of what cash outlays are normally needed to maintain a given level of sales, but they also need the help of their fellow executives. For example, if the purchasing department believes that commodity prices may soon be going up and plans to pick up several months' worth of raw material soon, the planner must know about it. If the marketing department is planning a major, expensive advertising campaign, the financial manager must be aware of its planned cost and timing. Normally, the financial manager will find most of this information in the profit budget or in later modifications of the budget, but this will not always be true. Every executive with the authority to commit large sums of money must be fully aware of the responsibility to keep the financial manager informed of future plans. Exhibit 3–3 shows estimated cash outflows included in the cash flow forecast.

Once cash inflows and disbursements have been forecast, the planner can forecast cash balances at the end of each planning unit. The results of this appear as the top and bottom lines of Exhibit 3–3. More detail on forecasting can be found in Chapter 4.

At this point, the planner has a cash flow *forecast*, not a *plan*. Planning is the mental process of visualizing a set of events that one is determined to make happen in the future, not just a summary of what one expects to happen. But it is at this stage that planning can begin. Some of the cash balances at the end of each planning interval may be higher than needed; others may be too low or even negative. Planners first decide how to cover temporary shortages of cash. Next, they decide how to invest any excess cash in order to earn the maximum return. The means of doing this are not limited to short-term borrowing and include delaying purchases or payments until a later period, deciding to reduce or eliminate certain expenditures, selling marketable securities or other assets, and accelerating collections. We discuss these in detail in later chapters.

Exhibit 3–4 shows the results of this kind of planning based on the cash flow forecast shown in Exhibit 3–3. The financial executive has decided to finance the forecast cash shortage in January by a $20,000 short-term bank loan with a yearly interest rate of 18 percent, which will be paid off in two equal installments in February and March. (The $19,400 actually received from the bank represents the loan less interest deducted in advance. This is known as a *discounted* loan.) By March, the company has spare cash, which it can invest in short-term, interest-yielding securities— $5,000 in each of the three months of March, April, and June.

However, this would have caused cash to drop to a low in May: $3,070 by the end of the month. Instead of investing less in April or borrowing again from the bank, the planner has decided that payment of some May bills can be deferred until June: $3,000 in professional fees and $2,000 for raw materials.

Thus, once the financial manager has determined how to invest excess cash and how to cover cash shortages, he or she incorporates the results of these decisions into the cash flow forecast, which now becomes a plan. The planner's remaining responsibility is to ensure, so far as is possible, that this plan is put into effect and is mirrored by actual results.

The accuracy of the forecasts that are used in preparing the cash flow plan is critical to having the plan be a useful tool. The less reliable the forecasts or the more uncertain the financial manager is about the unexpected events that may affect the cash flows, the larger the cash balances, or lines of credit, or both that are required. *GIGO* is an appropriate acronym in this case:

	January	February	March	April	May	June
Cash at start of month	$19,680	$ 9,380	$ 7,580	$ 7,580	$11,630	$ 8,070
Cash Inflows						
Sales receipts	$55,000	$57,000	$69,000	$61,000	$64,000	$65,000
Insurance claim					7,000	
Royalties on patent	4,000			3,500		
Short-term bank loan	19,400					
Total cash inflows	$78,400	$57,000	$69,000	$64,500	$71,000	$65,000
Cash Outflows						
Labor payroll	$23,000	$23,500	$24,000	$24,500	$31,000	$25,200
Salaries	4,800	4,800	4,800	5,600	5,600	5,600
Raw materials payments	31,000	15,500	18,250	11,650	26,760	17,625
Payments for supplies	2,400	1,800	2,000	2,000	2,000	2,000
Insurance			750			
Lease payments	1,000	1,000	1,500	1,000	1,000	1,500
Marketing expenses	500	500	1,500	500	500	500
Miscellaneous expenses	1,000	1,200	1,200	1,200	1,200	1,200
Dividends	18,000					
Income taxes	7,000			9,000		
Professional fees		500			1,000	3,000
New production equipment					5,500	
Bank loan repayments		10,000	10,000			
Purchase of marketable securities			5,000	5,000		5,000
Total cash outflows	$88,700	$58,800	$69,000	$60,450	$74,560	$61,625
Cash at end of month	$ 9,380	$ 7,580	$ 7,580	$11,630	$ 8,070	$11,445

Exhibit 3–4   Cash Flow Plan

garbage in, garbage out. If the planner does not have much confidence in the forecasts, the resulting plan will be of little value to the organization.

> ## Cash Flow Analysis
> ### and Planning

The previous section generally described how to perform a short-term forecast based on a receipts minus disbursement analysis. Though this is a commonly applied approach, you should recognize that much of the desired information is difficult to forecast since much of the receipt and disbursement data are not always available. This will surely complicate cash flow planning. Furthermore, the traditional receipts and disbursement approach does not lend itself easily to interpretations of cash flow. For example, the answers to such questions as how much the firm should set aside for investments in fixed assets or how the firm should fund future growth are not readily apparent from such an analysis.

In this section, we provide an overview of how cash flows can be calculated by an indirect method and an overview of the new Financial Accounting Standards Board (FASB) "Statement of Cash Flows." The new statement describes how cash flow actually comprises three cash components: cash from operations, cash from investments, and cash from financing. It also provides a nice format for interpreting and planning cash flows.

Although net cash flow can be calculated by subtracting cash disbursements from cash receipts, *cash flow from operations* is often calculated by taking net income and adding expenses that do not decrease net working capital (such as depreciation, amortization, and deferred taxes). Historically, financial managers used net income plus depreciation as a proxy for cash flow. This is no longer accepted behavior. Today, most accountants and financial managers recognize cash flow as being the former amount (net income plus expenses not decreasing net working capital) *plus* increases (minus decreases) in spontaneous liabilities *minus* increases (plus decreases) in spontaneous assets. Spontaneous assets and liabilities are those accounts that move directly with a change in sales. For example, accounts receivable and inventories would represent spontaneous assets, whereas accounts payable and accruals would indicate spontaneous liabilities.

CALCULATING
CASH FLOWS FROM
EXTERNAL DATA

This calculation of cash flows is referred to as an *indirect approach* since the actual cash receipts and disbursements are not used but are estimated from all the accounts affecting cash flows. For example, all the sources and uses of funds that affect cash flows from operations are included in the indirect cash flow calculation.

The indirect approach is frequently used for forecasting longer-term cash flows (one year and beyond) since projections of net income may receive greater attention than the actual timing of receipts and disbursements. The indirect approach may also facilitate more reliable long-term planning. A few examples using XYZ Corporation's balance sheet and income statement data illustrated in Exhibit 3–5 should make this clear.

Using the indirect approach, XYZ's cash from operations for 19X1 would be equal to:

Net income + depreciation + increases in deferred income tax +
increases in accounts payable + increases in accruals – increases in
accounts receivable – increases in inventories

Thus, cash flow from operations equals:

$250 + $400 + $100 + ($100 + $100) – ($200 + $300) = $450

You should recognize that notes payable are not included with the spontaneous liabilities. Notes payable do not move directly with changes in sales; they usually move as a residual account to offset temporary cash shortages. Thus, notes payable are not a spontaneous liability and are excluded from cash flow from operations calculations.

INCOME STATEMENTS
AT DECEMBER 31
(IN THOUSANDS OF DOLLARS)

	19X0	19X1
Net sales	$5,500	$6,500
Less cost of goods sold	3,800	4,100
Gross margin	$1,700	$2,400
Less depreciation expense	300	400
Less selling, general, and administrative	1,100	1,600
Income before taxes	$ 300	$ 400
Less income tax expense	100	150
Net income	$ 200	$ 250

BALANCE SHEETS
AT DECEMBER 31
(IN THOUSANDS OF DOLLARS)

	19X0	19X1
Cash	$ 500	$ 700
Marketable securities	1,000	1,100
Accounts receivable	750	950
Inventory	1,050	1,350
Total current assets	$3,300	$4,100
Fixed assets (net)	1,500	2,100
Total assets	$4,800	$6,200
Accounts payable	$ 600	$ 700
Accruals	150	250
Notes payable	250	450
Total current assets	$1,000	$1,400
Long-term debt	1,700	2,350
Deferred income taxes	200	300
Common stock	400	400
Additional paid-in capital	1,000	1,000
Retained earnings	500	750
Total assets	$4,800	$6,200

EXHIBIT 3–5   XYZ CORPORATION'S INCOME STATEMENTS AND BALANCE SHEETS

Although cash flow from operations was $450, the actual increase in cash and marketable securities was only $300 ($1,800 – $1,500). What do you suppose happened to the other $150? Much of the cash went toward expansion in fixed assets. In fact, the investment in fixed assets was $1,000. A good approximation in determining the investment in fixed assets is calculated by taking the difference in net fixed asset accounts and adding the current year's depreciation expense. In 19X1, the XYZ Corporation had a depreciation expense of $400. The depreciation expense plus the $600 change in net fixed assets ($2,100 – $1,500) equals $1,000 spent on net fixed assets for 19X1.

Since the firm had $450 in cash flow from 19X1 operations and in the same year spent $1,000 on net fixed assets, you may wonder how the firm was able to increase its cash and marketable securities balances by $300 ($1,800 − $1,500). The answer can be found in the considerable funds raised by borrowing bank debt. The XYZ Corporation borrowed an additional $650 in long-term debt and raised $200 in additional cash from short-term notes payable. Thus, from operations and net borrowings, the firm had total cash inflows of $1,300 ($450 + $850), yet spent only $1,000 on asset investments. Consequently, the firm had $300 left over to increase its cash and marketable securities accounts.

➤ FINANCIAL MANAGEMENT
 AND CASH FLOW PLANNING

Cash flow planning is one decision process that is taking place within the context of a much broader process (financial management) for companies. A way of thinking about cash flow management and its place in the broader concept of financial management that is consistent with financial theory is presented in a series of steps. It must be remembered that even though there appears to be a sequence of events associated with these steps, for most companies the steps are all going on at the same time.

Here are the steps in a company's financial management process:

1. Management decides what assets, current and long-term, it needs to acquire in order to carry out its line of business. Most of these decisions are carried out under some form of capital budgeting.
2. The financial (liability) structure of the company is determined by management, which desires to minimize the cost of capital of the company. The mix of debt and equity and the maturity of debt are key variables in this decision process.
3. Management decides on a target level of liquidity. This is done through cash flow planning.
4. Management compares its cash flow plan, financial structure, and capital budget to the actual state of the company. If the plans differ from actual, then cost-effective adjustments to move toward the targeted structure must be made.

Steps 1 and 2 determine the targeted structure of the company. They are the principal factors that affect the cash flow planner. In Exhibit 3–6, the structure of Company XYZ is based on consideration of steps 1 and 2.

Once management has determined the target levels of working capital, the cash flow planner's job is to bring the actual into line with the desired. How this is done is the subject matter of the remainder of this book.

In October 1987, the FASB issued a new "Statement of Cash Flows." This statement establishes standards for cash flow reporting and replaces the

STATEMENT OF
CASH FLOWS

	ACTUAL	DESIRED
Cash	$ 10	$ 15
Accounts receivable	100	80
Inventory	20	40
Fixed assets	180	180
Total assets	$310	$315
Accounts payable	$ 10	$ 25
Short-term borrowing	30	20
Long-term debt	120	120
Owner's equity	150	150
Total liabilities and equity	$310	$315

EXHIBIT 3–6   ACTUAL AND DESIRED FINANCIAL POSITION OF COMPANY XYZ

statement of changes in financial position in the set of financial statements. In addition, the new statement of cash flows classifies each of the cash flows by operating, investing, and financing activities. Cash flow from operations can be calculated either directly or indirectly as shown above.

Cash flows from investing activities include purchases (or proceeds from disposal) of property, plant, and equipment; acquisitions of companies; purchases (or proceeds from sale) of investment securities; or loans made (or collections on loans). Cash flows from financing activities include proceeds of short-term debt (or payments to settle short-term debt), proceeds of long-term debt, payments on capital lease obligations, proceeds from issuing common stock, or dividends paid. The net sum of cash flows from operations plus cash flows from investing activities plus cash flows from financing activities equals the change in the cash balance. Typically, a firm would have a positive cash inflow from operations and a negative cash outflow from investing activities. The net flow from financing and the resultant change in the cash balance depends on the difference between the operating flows and the investing flows. The example illustrated with data from Exhibit 3–5 is shown as follows:

Net cash flow from operating activities:	
Net income	$ 250
Noncash expenses, revenues, losses, and gains included in income:	
Depreciation	$ 400
Deferred taxes	100
Net increase in receivables, inventory, and payables	(300)
Net cash flow from operating activities	$ 450
Cash flows from investing activities:	
Cash outflows for property, plant, and equipment	$(1,000)
Net cash used by investing activities	$(1,000)
Cash flows from financing activities:	
Proceeds from short-term debt	$ 200
Proceeds from long-term debt	650
Net cash provided by financing activities	$ 850
Net increase (decrease) in cash	$ 300

Note how the change in cash (and marketable securities) is the same as before. However, with the new approach we see clearly how the firm is generating an increase in cash.

Although the firm has a net cash flow from operating activities of $450, the cash flows from investing activities ($1,000) more than off-set this amount. If cash flows from financing activities were less than $550, the cash balance actually would have dropped. However, the amount bor-rowed was in fact $850, leaving an excess of borrowed funds of $300 that went into the cash reservoir.

The FASB approach lends itself easily to analyzing current and future cash flows. For example, firms experiencing high growth levels would be expected to have larger investments in property, plant, and equipment as well as growing investments in accounts receivable and inventories. Con-sequently, the firm would be expected to borrow more from institutional sources so as not to deplete the cash reserves. This is consistent with the matching concept discussed in Chapter 2. Alternatively, some managers may try to minimize borrowing levels by *not* reinvesting in property, plant, and equipment. This can have far-reaching consequences on future cash flows and may distort the existing quality of profits and total cash flows.

➤ FREE CASH FLOW
AND UNDEDICATED
CASH FLOW

Many financial analysts and managers are becoming increasingly interested in a concept called free cash flow. *Free cash flow* is equal to cash flow from operations minus investments in capital expenditures that are required to maintain the company's competitiveness. In the example cited above, XYZ's free cash flow would be a negative $550 ($450 – $1,000). This implies that the firm does not have surplus funds from operations since they are in fact borrowing in order to maintain appropriate levels of capi-tal investments.

Another term that is becoming more common is pretax undedicated cash flow. *Undedicated cash flow* is equal to free cash flow plus tax plus interest expense. Undedicated cash flow, or "raider" cash flow, is emerging as an important variable in appraising the investment attrac-tion of engaging in leveraged buyouts, restructuring, and mergers of publicly owned companies. Prospective buyers (raiders) often add back interest and taxes so that they can get the broadest possible picture of the company's available cash. Then the investors determine how they could redirect the cash flows. Since the prospective buyers are going to be own-ers and not passive shareholders, they are more concerned about having control of the cash than about operating profits. Often, much of the oper-ating cash flow is devoted to servicing debt after the transaction. As the firm begins to service the debt arrangement, the equity in the company automatically grows.

➤ The Cash
Conversion Cycle

The concept of the cash conversion cycle is important in working capital management. The cash conversion cycle of a firm is the time period that elapses from the point when the company makes a cash outlay to purchase raw materials to the point when cash is collected from the sale of finished products. Cash turnover represents the number of times that the firm's cash is converted into a marketable product and back into cash.

In applying the cash conversion cycle mode, it is useful to first define the following terms:

1. *Inventory conversion period*—the average length of time required to convert raw material into finished goods and then to sell these goods.
2. *Receivables conversion period*—the average length of time required to convert the firm's receivables into cash. The receivables conversion period is synonymous with the average collection period.
3. *Payables deferral period*—the average length of time between the purchase of raw materials and the cash payment for these materials.

The cash conversion cycle is equal to the inventory conversion period plus the receivables conversion period minus the payables deferral period. As an illustration of the conversion cycle, consider the following example:

The JMS Corporation purchases all its raw materials on a credit basis and sells all its finished goods on credit. The firm calculates that it is taking 30 days on average to pay its accounts payable and 40 days on average to collect its accounts receivable. In addition, 50 days on average elapse between the purchase of raw materials and the sale of finished goods. The cash conversion cycle for the JMS Corporation is equal to the inventory conversion period of 50 days plus the receivables conversion period of 40 days minus the payables deferral period of 30 days, or a total of 60 days.

The objective of the firm is to reduce the cash conversion cycle as much as possible without harming the firm's operations. This improves the firm's profits because the longer the cash conversion cycle, the greater the need for external financing. Therefore, shortening the cash conversion cycle reduces the costs associated with external financing. The cash conversion cycle can be reduced by (1) shortening the inventory conversion period through processing and selling the firm's output more quickly, (2) shortening the receivables conversion period through speeding up the collection of receivables, and (3) lengthening the payables deferral period through slowing down payments to suppliers.

The cash turnover is calculated by dividing the cash conversion cycle into 360. For the example given above, JMS Corporation would have a cash turnover of 6 (360 ÷ 60). The greater a company's cash turnover, the less cash the firm requires. Therefore, the firm should attempt to maximize its cash turnover.

The major objective of cash management is to operate the company in a fashion that requires the minimum level of cash. The lower the amount of cash invested in operations, the greater the availability of surplus cash that can be invested in short-term marketable securities or used to repay debts. On the other hand, the greater the level of cash required for the firm's operations, the more investment opportunities the firm must forgo. Thus, the fewer interest-earning assets the firm can acquire due to cash needed for operations, the higher the opportunity cost of cash.

The minimum operating cash can be computed by dividing the firm's total annual outlays by its cash turnover. For example, if JMS Corporation spends $20 million annually on operating outlays and has a cash turnover of 4, its minimum operating cash is $5 million ($20 million/4). If the firm begins the year with $5 million in cash, it should have sufficient cash to pay bills as they come due. If the firm could earn 8 percent on short-term investments, its opportunity cost of maintaining a $5 million cash balance is $400,000 (.08 × $5 million).

➤ SUMMARY

In this chapter, we described two different ways to calculate cash flow from operations, and we provided a summary of the new FASB "Statement of Cash Flows." We also discussed ways to interpret cash flows and how to plan for future activity. The importance of cash flow should be clear. A shortage of cash flow could result in the loss of valuable trade discounts or, in extreme circumstances, financial embarrassment and bankruptcy. A surplus of liquidity does not necessarily translate into greater returns to shareholders, but it certainly provides opportunities for prospective buyers who understand how to utilize positive cash flows. The caveat for interpreting cash flow is the same as that used for net income: Quality counts. This means that firms that depend heavily on depreciation to generate cash flow are not looked on as favorably as firms that have a preponderance of cash flow from operations. Furthermore, cash flow should be analyzed to make certain that the firm is investing properly in order to maintain future operations. Managers who attempt to improve cash flow artificially by ignoring necessary investments in property, plant, and equipment may not be familiar with the concepts of free cash flow or undedicated cash flow. These definitions should help assess the perceived value of a company's worth.

CHAPTER 4

FORECASTING CASH FLOW

By the end of this chapter, the reader will be able to:

LEARNING OBJECTIVES

1. Identify the two approaches to cash flow forecasting.
2. Identify the objectives of cash flow forecasting.
3. Understand the use of pro forma statements in cash flow forecasting.
4. Be able to generate a cash flow forecast using the receipts and disbursements approach.
5. Identify various methods for forecasting.

The main financial goal of management is to maximize shareholder wealth. To achieve this aim, managers must have a financial plan. One of the major components of the company's financial plan is a cash budget based upon the cash flow cycle. In order to develop a workable financial plan, a forecast of future cash flows is needed.

Cash forecasting is extremely important to all organizations. It enables the manager to anticipate periods when the company may be faced with a shortage or surplus of cash. The identification of the amount and the timing of these surpluses or shortages constitutes the cash forecast. What is done to finance the shortages and invest the surplus or manage the amount and timing of the cash flow is what constitutes the cash flow plan.

➤ TYPES OF CASH FLOW
FORECASTS

The cash flow forecast is not the only type of forecast that managers must make as part of their financial planning. Indeed, many of these other forecasts serve as input into the cash flow forecast. The manager's capital budget is a detailed forecast of the amounts and timing of cash flows associated with capital expenditures or the acquisition of productive assets. The production plan is a forecast of expected expenses associated with the conversion of raw materials into finished goods. The sales forecast is a forecast of when the finished goods will be sold. Each of these forecasts is usually completed prior to the cash flow forecast because the forecasts serve as inputs into the cash flow forecast.

The type of cash flow forecast used by a particular company can be differentiated by two factors: time and forecasting approach. With respect to time, the company is faced with three problems: long-range, medium-range, and short-term. The cash flow forecast can be made over periods of various lengths: yearly flows, quarterly flows, monthly flows, weekly flows, and daily flows. It is possible to start with daily flows and aggregate the forecast into weekly or monthly periods. This is called scheduling. Another approach is to start with aggregate figures, for example, for a year and subdivide the forecast into monthly, weekly, or daily flows. This is called distribution.

Additionally, with respect to time, a cash flow forecast of one or more years is considered long-range. The primary purpose of this forecast is to assess the company's long-range financing and operating policies. A typical long-range forecast could go out five or ten years with annual updates. It would include information on capital investments, company dividend policy, mergers and acquisitions, and divestitures. Any strategic actions that the managers can foresee in the next ten years is appropriate for inclusion in the long-range forecast.

A medium-term cash flow forecast would normally be for one year either in quarterly or monthly time intervals. It is based on a business-as-usual assumption with no changes to capital structure or asset base. It is generally based on accounting information that has been adjusted to reflect accruals and deferrals. The main purpose of this cash budget is to determine short-term financing requirements and/or short-term marketable security investment activities. It can also be used as a standard for comparing actual performance to expected performance in an evaluation framework.

A daily—or, for large companies, hourly—cash flow budget is used to determine the actual availability of cash inflows and the loss of cash outflows so that the cash manager can schedule cash transfers from concentration accounts and fund disbursement accounts, and have information for very short-term borrowing and/or investing decisions.

Each of these three types of cash budgets has unique forecasting problems associated with their formulation. The long-term budget is difficult to forecast because of changes in the financial or economic environment which cannot be foreseen. The daily budget is difficult to forecast because of unexpected random events that can have large affects on the flow of cash through the system. For example, an unexpected snowstorm could slow down or close transportation systems that are used for the processing or clearing of funds. Different forecasting methods will be discussed that may be more appropriate for one type of cash flow budget than another.

A final way of classifying cash forecasts is to look at the way the cash flows are determined. The daily cash budget uses the receipts and disbursements approach. The timing and amount of cash flowing in or out of the company over some forecasting period must be identified. Every dollar of cash is kept under close control. This approach is ideal for relatively short time periods (i.e., daily or weekly and for short time horizons, and quarterly or up to one year). A typical form of such a cash flow forecast is shown in Exhibit 4–1.

	MONDAY	TUESDAY	WEDNESDAY	... ...
Beginning Cash Balance	_____	_____	_____	_____
Plus receipts	_____	_____	_____	_____
Cash sales	_____	_____	_____	_____
Collection of receivables	_____	_____	_____	_____
Borrowing	_____	_____	_____	_____
Sale of assets	_____	_____	_____	_____
...	_____	_____	_____	_____
Minus disbursements:				
Payments for wages, salaries, inventories, etc.	_____	_____	_____	_____
Interest payments	_____	_____	_____	_____
Dividends	_____	_____	_____	_____
Tax payments	_____	_____	_____	_____
...	_____	_____	_____	_____
Equals ending cash balance	══════	══════	══════	══════

EXHIBIT 4–1   CASH FORECAST OF RECEIPTS AND DISBURSEMENTS

SOURCES OF FUNDS		USE OF FUNDS
Net income		Finance a deficit from operations
Depreciation		Dividends
Increases in liabilities		Decrease in liabilities
Decrease in assets (except cash)		Increases in assets (except cash)
Total sources	−	Total uses
	=	Change in cash

EXHIBIT 4–2   ADJUSTED NET INCOME APPROACH TO CASH FLOW FORECASTING

The medium- and long-term cash budgets, although they could be generated by scheduling, are normally prepared using the adjusted income statement approach. In this case, the cash flow forecaster begins with the pro forma income statement and makes the appropriate adjustments to change it from an accrual statement to a cash basis. This method is based upon examining changes to asset and liability accounts with the cash account serving as the residual or balancing account. This approach is particularly helpful to the long-range or strategic planner interested in answering that "what-if" question. For example: What if we purchase a new technology for our production process? What, then, is the impact on the asset and liability structure of the company? Exhibit 4–2 shows a format for this approach.

For the remainder of this chapter, the cash receipts and disbursements method will be emphasized. However, it should be remembered that some

---

Income Statement

Sales	$30
Cost of goods sold	15
Depreciation	5
Fixed costs	5
Interest	2
Earnings before taxes	3
Taxes (33%)	1
Net income after tax	$ 2

Balance Sheet

Cash	$ 2	A/P	$15
A/R	5	Long-term debt	9
Inventory	10	Equity	3
Fixed assets	17	Retained earnings	7
Total assets	$34	Total liabilities and equity	$34

Exhibit 4–3   Company ABC's Financial Statements, October 19X1

very useful information can be generated from the net income approach. Cash managers should be aware of the information available from both approaches in order to make better decisions.

➤ Objectives of
Cash Flow Forecasting

The basic purpose of forecasting cash flows is to provide information to the cash manager so that he or she can plan for the cash that will be necessary to conduct the business of the company, be it long-term or short-term in nature. One major objective of cash flow management is to increase the return on the company's marketable securities investment and/or reduce the cost of securing short-term funds. Errors in the forecast could cause the company to invest its surplus cash in financial instruments with shorter maturities than necessary, thereby giving up some additional return. Likewise, errors could place the company into the embarrassing and costly situation of having unexpectedly to arrange for short-term financing.

By forecasting and planning for the orderly flow of cash through the company, the cash flow manager can control what is happening to the company. As a fallout, the information about an unexpected cash shortage or surplus can be an indication of changes in the environment in which the company does business. This signal needs to be evaluated by management in order to achieve an understanding of what is happening. Other objectives of cash flow forecasting include:

☐ Identifying seasonal or cyclical fluctuations in business activity.
☐ Identifying amount and timing of major cash outflows to meet tax payments, maturing bond issues, dividend payments, etc.
☐ Identifying amount and timing of major cash outflows associated with growth and expansion.
☐ Identifying amount and timing of cash shortage so that financing can be arranged in an orderly cost-effective fashion.
☐ Identifying amount and timing of surplus cash for investment.
☐ Coordinating the activities of subsidiaries and branches of the organization.
☐ Permitting the company to take advantage of discounts or bargain purchases, should the opportunity arise.

> ## Cash Flow Items to be
> ## Forecast for
> ## Net Income Approach

The cash flow forecast will require an estimate of cash inflows and cash outflows. Basically, we have three approaches that can be used to forecast the levels of the various accounts on the cash flow statement. As a matter of course, we probably should use all three methods to forecast each account, but after the analyst has gained some experience, certain methods become preferred when forecasting certain accounts. The three methods are:

1. Accounting definition
2. Ratio relationship
3. Management policy

The first, accounting definition, is probably the easiest to understand. The level of taxable income in a given period that must be forecasted is simply taxable revenue minus allowable expenses and deductions. Once the various revenue, expense, and deduction accounts have been forecasted, the forecast of taxable income is always determined according to IRS and accounting definitions. This leads us to the question: How are the forecasts for revenues, expenses, and deductions made?

The answer to this question is: Use the second method of ratio or inherent business connection between certain accounts. For example, the level of forecasted interest payments depends on the amount of borrowing and the interest rate. The level of depreciation expense depends upon the type and amount of depreciable plant and equipment and IRS rules. The cash flow from the collection of accounts receivables depends upon the company's credit policy and the amount of credit rates.

Company ABC currently is in a position shown by the financial statements in Exhibit 4–3. Management may have stipulated certain policies or guidelines that affect the level of cash required for a given period of operation. Things such as minimum cash levels or minimum levels of inven-

PRO FORMA INCOME STATEMENT

Sales	$ 33	[10% growth on current sales level.]
Cost of goods sold	16.5	⎡Historically, cost of goods sold/sales = $15/$30 = 50%: 50% × 33 = $16.5⎤
Depreciation	5	⎡Depreciable assets + purchases of depreciable assets − sales of depreciable assets = depreciable assets for forecasted period: 17 + 3 − 0 = $20 Depending on the type and life of the depreciable assets, IRS rules must be followed to determine the level of depreciation expense. In this case we assume it to be $5.⎤
Fixed costs	5	⎡Assume to be unaffected by new level of activity.⎤
Interest	1.92	⎡Interest/Total Liabilities = 2/24 = 8.33%. We expect long-term debt to decrease by $1 so total liabilities may go down to $23. This assumes current liabilities remain the same. At this point this may or may not be a valid assumption. Interest = Total liabilities × Interest rate $1.92 = 23 × .0833⎤
Earnings before tax	4.58	
Taxes (33%)	1.51	
Net income after tax	3.07	
Less dividends	1	
Increase in retained earnings	$ 2.07	

A

Exhibit continued on next page.

EXHIBIT 4–4 COMPANY ABC'S PRO FORMA FINANCIAL STATEMENT, OCTOBER 19X1

tory must be considered when forecasting the cash inflow and outflow for the company. An illustration of each of these approaches is included in the following simple example.

During the forecasted period, sales are expected to increase by 10 percent. New equipment costing $3 will be purchased for cash. There will be no new long-term debt issues, and $1 of old long-term debt must be paid off. Dividends totalling $1 will be paid. Management has stated a policy that cash will be maintained at a level of $4. There are no other expected changes from current operations. Our task is to develop a cash flow forecast based on this information.

The first step is to develop a pro forma financial statement based on the information at hand. The pro forma financial statements along with supporting calculations and assumptions are presented in Exhibit 4–4.

A few words about the pro forma statements in Exhibit 4–4 are in order before we use this information to determine our cash inflow and outflow statement. On the pro forma income statement, we estimated the interest

EXHIBIT 4–4   *Continued from previous page.*

PRO FORMA BALANCE SHEET

(4) Cash [Management policy] $ 4   (9) A/P $\begin{bmatrix} \text{Total assets} - \\ \text{L/T debt} - \text{equity} \\ - \text{retained earnings} = \text{A/P} \\ 40.5 - 8 - 3 - \\ 9.07 = \$20.43 \end{bmatrix}$ $20.43

(5) A/R $\begin{bmatrix} \text{Sales/AR} = 30/5 = 6 \\ \text{If there are no} \\ \text{changes in the credit} \\ \text{and collection policies} \\ \text{of the company and} \\ \text{if customer payment} \\ \text{habits remain} \\ \text{unchanged, then we} \\ \text{can forecast next} \\ \text{year's A/R as:} \\ 6 = 33/[\text{A/R}] \\ \text{A/R} = \$5.5 \end{bmatrix}$ 5.5

(6) Inventory 11
$\begin{bmatrix} \text{Sales/inventory} = 30/10 = 3 \\ \text{If there is no change in the} \\ \text{way the company produces} \\ \text{or distributes its product,} \\ \text{then we can forecast} \\ \text{next year's inventory as:} \\ 3 = 33/\text{Inventory} \\ \text{Inventory} = 11 \end{bmatrix}$

(3) Long-term debt 8
[Old ± changes: 9 – 1]
Total liabilities $28.43

(2) Equity [No change] 3

(1) Retained earnings 7 + 2.07 9.07
$\begin{bmatrix} \text{Current level} + \text{expected} \\ \text{increase from pro forma} \\ \text{income statement} \end{bmatrix}$

(7) Fixed assets 20
$\begin{bmatrix} \text{Old} + \text{Purchases} - \text{Sales} \\ 17 + 3 - 0 = 20 \end{bmatrix}$

Total assets (8) $40.5   Total liabilities + equity $40.5

The circled numbers 1 through 9 indicate the order of estimating the various accounts. 1 indicates retained earnings are estimated first from the old balance sheet and pro forma income statement.

B

expense based on the assumption that total liabilities would be $23. After we have completed the pro forma balance sheet, we see that the total liabilities are in fact estimated to be $28.43. This being the case, our assumption of $23 for the purpose of calculating interval is not correct. Therefore, at this stage of the forecast, we would go back and change the interest expense to $2.31 (.08333 × 27.8). However, this change will affect the taxable income, taxes, and retained earnings on the pro forma income statement. These changes will then affect the pro forma balance sheet. It is appropriate to redo the pro forma balance sheet to reflect these changes. The pro forma statements incorporating these changes is presented in Exhibit 4–5.

Pro Forma Income Statement

Sales	$33
Cost of goods sold	16.5
Depreciation	5
Fixed costs	5
Interest	2.31
Earnings before tax	4.19
Taxes (33%)	1.39
Net Income	2.8
Less dividends	1
Increase in retained earnings	$ 1.8

A

Pro Forma Balance Sheet

Cash	$ 4	A/P	$20.7]*
A/R	5.5	Long-term debt	8
Inventory	11	Equity	3
Fixed assets	20	Retained earnings	8.8
Total assets	$40.5	Total liabilities + equity	$40.5

*Note the level of total liabilities is now $28.7; the amount of interest expense was determined based on a level of total liabilities of $27.8. Therefore, the interest expense may still be understated. However, in this case not by an amount that will have a significant impact on the forecast.

B

Exhibit 4–5   Company ABC's Revised Pro Forma Statement

Using the revised pro forma statements in Exhibit 4–5 we are now ready to generate a cash flow statement using the format developed in Exhibit 4–2. The forecasted cash flow statement for Company ABC is shown in Exhibit 4–6.

➤ Cash Flow Items to be Forecast for Receipts and Disbursements Approach

For the receipts and disbursements cash forecasting method shown in Exhibit 4–1, estimates need to be made of the many transactions by which the company collects and pays each day. The greater the breakdown with respect to individual types of transactions, the more accurate the forecast. However, costs in terms of time and money will increase as individual transactions are increased.

As a first step, the receipts and disbursements should be separated into two groups: nonrepetitive cash flows and recurring cash flows. By nonre-

SOURCES OF FUNDS		CLASS OF FUNDS	
Net income	$ 2.8	Finance a deficit	
Depreciation	5	Dividends	$ 1
Increases in liabilities		Decreases in liabilities	0
(New – Old)		Increases in assets (except cash)	9.5
(28.7 – 24)	4.7		
Decreases in assets (except cash)	0	(Purchases = New + Depreciation – Old)	
		9.5 = 36.5 + 5 – 32	
Total sources	$12.5 —	Total uses	$10.5

EXHIBIT 4–6 PRO FORMA CASH FLOW STATEMENTS FOR COMPANY ABC

petitive cash flows we mean easily forecastable, relatively large cash flows such as tax payments, dividend payments, bond interest payments, lease payments, construction or major asset acquisition payments, receipt of proceeds from a bond or stock issue, and receipt from sale of an asset, division, and/or business. This list is not exhaustive but is meant to give an idea that these cash flows are usually known in advance, and they are not a normal repetitive part of the cash flow cycle.

The recurring cash flows can be thought of as those cash flows that are associated with the normal business operations of the company. Examples are: the payments made for the purchase of raw materials, workers' salaries, maintenance, payroll taxes, utility bills, and the receipts generated from cash sales or the collection of such items as accounts receivables, rental receipts, and royalties.

Next, the inflows and outflows should be dealt with separately, because the timing and statistical properties of inflows is probably very different from that of outflows.

In most cases, the fluctuations of inflows and outflows can be identified with such factors as sales, economic conditions, and management policies or decisions. Such variables identify the operating environment for business activity, and these variables are all associated with some degree of uncertainty. Thus, one of the objectives of cash flow forecasting will be to identify the causes and reduce the amount of uncertainty, or have the planner prepare to meet unavoidable variations. Hence, quantitative or statistical techniques have proven to be very useful in cash forecasting. We now turn our attention to the various tools and techniques that can be used to help in forecasting cash flows.

➤ WHY DO CASH FLOWS FLUCTUATE?

The timing and amounts of cash inflows and outflows are primarily affected by five factors:

1. *Level of sales.* The timing and amounts of receipts and disbursements

are closely tied to fluctuations in sales. For example, cash collections from accounts receivable can be expected to increase shortly after credit sales have experienced an increase. Additionally, as sales increase, the amount of money spent in paying for new inventories and workers' salaries can also be expected to increase.

2. *Seasonal fluctuations.* Depending on the type of product and the line of business, the sales forecast may be highly seasonal; think of toys as an example. In the fall, the toy company will experience large seasonal disbursements as it pays the bills incurred in building up its inventories for Christmas sales. The receipts will be highly seasonal also, as the cash receipts are collected after the first of the year.

3. *Cyclical fluctuations.* As nation or worldwide economic conditions change, the level of sales will also respond, thereby affecting the amounts of receipts and disbursements. As the economy moves into a recessionary period, we would expect sales to fall off, which would lead to lower receipts and disbursements. Similarly, as the economy moves into an expansionary period, we would expect the increase in sales to lead to higher receipts and disbursements.

4. *Changes in the technological environment.* Most businesses can be defined in a technological framework. If new technologies of production or distribution are introduced, we would expect the level of sales to be affected, and also the relationship between the timing of the cash receipts and disbursements and the actual sale. For example, if a new and more efficient production machine is brought on line, the level of inventories may be reduced, thereby reducing the costs and disbursements associated with carrying inventory.

5. *Management policies.* The philosophy and policies of management are a major determinant on the amount and timing of cash flows. Differing credit terms will lead to different sales levels and different receipt patterns of cash flow. The use of JIT inventory will change the disbursement pattern of cash outflows.

➤ Making Forecasts for Daily Cash Flows

In order to be able to forecast the timing and levels of cash flowing into and out of the company, the analysts must have a thorough understanding of the information flows and the cash processing flows within their companies. Knowledge of the external environment is also crucial, because the speed of inflows can be greatly affected by external factors. The speed of outflows may also be affected, but not to the same degree as inflows. Using the time line concept developed in Chapter 2, we can generate a framework for analyzing cash inflows and outflows, which is of great help to the person asked to forecast future flows. A simple example will illustrate this use of the time line. In Exhibit 4–7, we show the time line associated with the purchase of potatoes by a fast food restaurant.

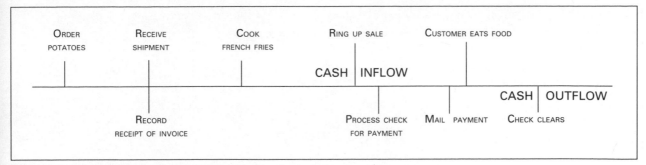

EXHIBIT 4–7   TIME LINE FOR FORECASTING CASH OUTFLOWS AND INFLOWS

The fast food restaurant specializes in french fried potatoes. Given an efficient inventory ordering system, it is possible for the restaurant to receive and process the potatoes and sell them for cash before it has to pay for them. The processing is shown by the top half of the time line in Exhibit 4–7. The handling of payment for the potatoes is shown by the lower half of the time line. After the forecaster has diagrammed the process and the cash flow, he is in a position to identify what kinds of information or factors that will affect future cash flows.

Information from the ordering department as to the frequency and size of orders would help the forecasters get an idea of the frequency and timing. The payables department could provide information on the receipt of invoices. By knowing the credit terms of the supplier and the company's payment policies, the forecaster could estimate when the check will clear the bank. Daily receipts for food sold would also be useful information. Based on the recurring patterns of cash flow generated by this process, the forecaster is now in a position to ascertain if there is a daily, weekly, or monthly pattern to the cash flow. Information should be collected from the above departments over a reasonable and representative time period. Unusual events such as holidays, bad weather, or good weather should also be considered in formulating the initial ideas of the cash flow. The past time period over which the information is collected should not be too long, because fundamental changes could have taken place that will affect the timing of the cash flows. If there has been a change (for example, a new restaurant opens across the street), then historical data may not reflect what is going to happen in the future.

➤ METHODS OF CASH FLOW
FORECASTING (THE BASICS)

Each of the receipts and disbursements associated with the daily cash flow forecast can be viewed as a variable. To assist in visualizing what we mean by a variable, we can use the concept of a probability distribution. A probability distribution is defined as a range of estimates of the likelihood of the occurrence of various future outcomes. For example, a company expects to receive cash sales of $100,000 a week, but this may vary as low as $75,000 or as high as $125,000. The mean or expected value can be defined as the most

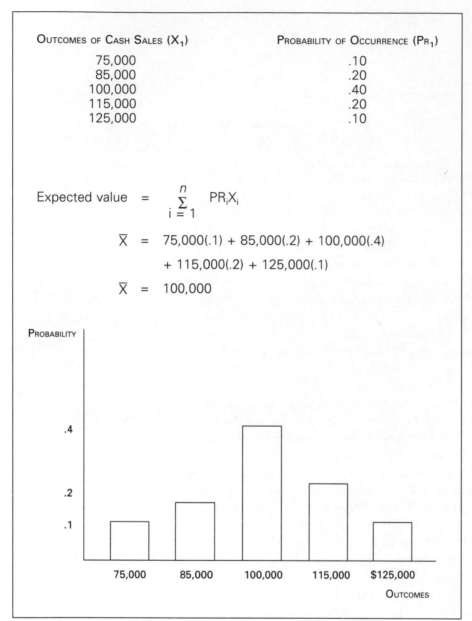

Outcomes of Cash Sales (X_1)	Probability of Occurrence (PR_1)
75,000	.10
85,000	.20
100,000	.40
115,000	.20
125,000	.10

Expected value $= \sum_{i=1}^{n} PR_i X_i$

$\overline{X} = 75{,}000(.1) + 85{,}000(.2) + 100{,}000(.4)$
$+ 115{,}000(.2) + 125{,}000(.1)$

$\overline{X} = 100{,}000$

Exhibit 4–8   Probability Distribution

likely or average forecast of the cash inflow. Exhibit 4–8 shows the probabilities and outcomes associated with this company's forecast.

The distribution shown in Exhibit 4–8 is called a "discrete probability distribution." Discrete because it only allows for five outcomes. It is not very likely that if one were forecasting weekly cash sales that only five levels of sales would be possible. A more realistic forecast would allow for a large number of cash sales levels between some minimum and maximum. This is called a continuous probability distribution and is shown in Exhibit 4–9.

The distribution shown in Exhibit 4–9 is a useful way of representing our forecast. It conveys information about the maximum ($125,000), the

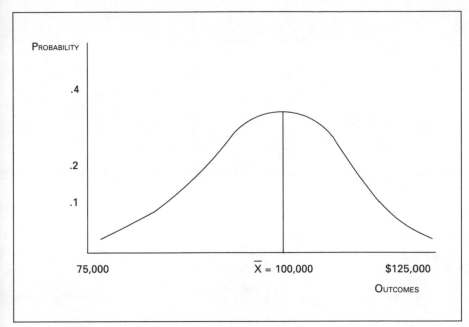

PROBABILITY

.4

.2

.1

75,000   X̄ = 100,000 $125,000

OUTCOMES

EXHIBIT 4-9   CONTINUOUS PROBABILITY DISTRIBUTION

minimum ($75,000), and the most likely level of cash sales ($100,000). The probability distribution highlights the fact that a single forecasted value is a point estimate. For example, if one were to forecast a cash sales level of $98,352.28, we could ask: What is the probability or chance that the actual cash sales level would equal exactly this amount? The answer is: It is not very likely (zero or low probability) that our point estimate forecast will be realized exactly. On the other hand, if we were to forecast that our cash sales level were to be between $75,000 and $125,000, more likely than not there is a 100 percent probability that the actual level of cash sales will fall within this range.

The major importance of the probability distribution concept is that it highlights the fact that a cash forecast is not a point estimate; it is not a single number. Rather, a forecast will be an expected value or center point of a range of possible cash inflows. In this case, we expect the cash sales to be around $100,000, but they could be as low as $75,000 or as high as $125,000. The spread or range of values is also a useful concept when one is making a forecast. In Exhibit 4–10 we show two different forecasts with the same expected value. One forecast (II) ranges from $50,000 to $150,000, while our initial forecast (I) ranges from $75,000 to $125,000.

Looking at the two forecasts in Exhibit 4–10, we clearly can see they are different. Even though they both have the same expected value of $100,000, forecast II has the possibility of being as low as $50,000 or as high as $150,000. This wider range is associated with greater instability or wider fluctuations. At this point, we need a statistical measure to distinguish between forecast I and II. The measure that is used is called the standard deviation.

A standard deviation is defined as a measure of the dispersion of values that approximate a normal probability distribution. A normal probability

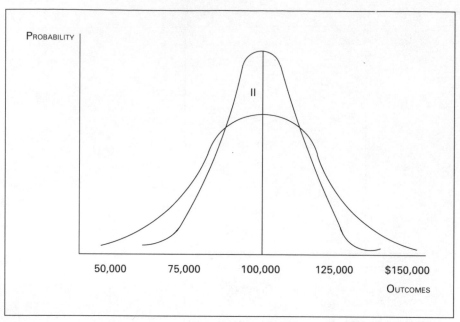

PROBABILITY

II

50,000   75,000   100,000   125,000 $150,000

OUTCOMES

EXHIBIT 4-10   DIFFERENT RANGES FOR FORECASTS

distribution is the bell-shaped curve that we've seen in Exhibits 4–9 and 4–10. A small standard deviation indicates a small range of possible outcomes and identifies a forecast with smaller fluctuations similar to forecast I in Exhibit 4–10. The usefulness of the standard deviation as a measure of range or dispersion is the following fact: For a normal distribution, the entire range of outcomes is covered by six standard deviations: three above the mean or expected value and three below. Therefore, the highest value of a range will be three standard deviations above the mean and the lowest value will be three standard deviations below the mean.

Based on the forecast for the level of cash sales used in Exhibit 4–8, we can calculate the standard deviation as shown in Exhibit 4–11.

In addition to specifying the entire range of possible values, the standard deviation (σ) can be used to determine the likelihood or probability of achieving a range of values. We have tables that provide the probability of occurrence for different ranges associated with the normal curve. Exhibit 4–12 shows the relationship between probability of occurrence and standard deviation.

From Exhibit 4–12 we can see that 68 percent of all values occur within plus or minus one standard deviation of the mean. Half or 34 percent occur between the mean and plus one standard deviation; the other half or 34 percent occur between the mean and minus one standard deviation. Hence, outcomes close to the mean are more likely to occur than extreme values. The relationship shown in Exhibit 4–12 can be handled for any normal distribution using a standard normal distribution table. Exhibit 4–13 is an example of such a table. As an example of the use of such a table, we can look at our cash sales forecast of $100,000 expected value (mean) with a standard deviation of $14,660, and

OUTCOMES OF CASH SALES (X_i)	PROBABILITY OF OCCURRENCE (PR_i)	$(X_i - \overline{X})^2$	$(X_i - \overline{X})^2 PR_i$
$ 75,000	.1	625,000,000	62,500,000
85,000	.2	225,000,000	45,000,000
100,000	.4	0	0
115,000	.2	225,000,000	45,000,000
125,000	.1	625,000,000	62,500,000

$$\sigma^2 \quad = \quad 215,000,000$$

$$\overline{X} = \$100,000 \qquad \sigma \quad = \quad \sqrt{215,000,000}$$

$$\text{Standard deviation} \quad = \quad \sigma \quad = \quad 14,660$$

$$\sigma = \sqrt{\sum_{i=1}^{n} (X_i - \overline{X})^2 Pr_i}$$

EXHIBIT 4-11 THE STANDARD DEVIATION

ask the question: What is the chance (probability) that the cash sales will be below $85,340? The answer to this is shown in Exhibit 4–14.

The expected value, standard deviation, and normal probability distribution are concepts that help us visualize forecasted cash flows. We now turn our attention to other statistical methods based on these concepts that will allow us to measure the accuracy of our forecasts.

➤ METHODS OF FORECASTING

A general method or model for forecasting cash flows can be stated as:

$$CF = \alpha + \beta_1 F_1 + \beta_2 F_2 \ldots$$

where:

CF is the cash flow to be forecast.

α is a constant term unaffected by the other factors (F_i).

F_i are factors called explanatory variables that are related to the level of cash flow.

Any forecast of CF is subject to error because of the uncertainty about the future values of the factors (F_i) and the uncertainty about the relationship between the F_i and CF or the βs (betas). We will look at four applications of this general linear forecasting model:

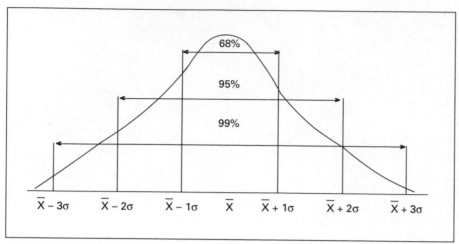

EXHIBIT 4–12   PROBABILITY OF OCCURRENCE AND STANDARD DEVIATION

NUMBER OF σ FROM MEAN	PERCENTAGE OF VALUES BETWEEN MEAN AND + σ
.1	3.98
.5	19.15
1.0	34.13
1.5	43.32
2.0	47.72
2.5	49.38
3.0	49.87

EXHIBIT 4–13   STANDARD NORMAL DISTRIBUTION TABLE

1. The constant forecast.
2. Ratio forecast.
3. Growth.
4. Dependency on multiple factors.

The constant factor application of the general model assumes that the cash flow (CF) is only related to α and none of the other factors or:

$$CF = \alpha$$

For example, if the company had signed a lease agreement that called for lease payments of $15,000 per month for the next year, this cash outflow would be forecasted as $15,000 with complete certainty every month. Here we are assuming that the company intends to honor the lease agreement. Other examples of contractual payments such as interest or principal payments associated with matters like debt, fixed payments for rentals, and declared dividend payments can be handled in this manner.

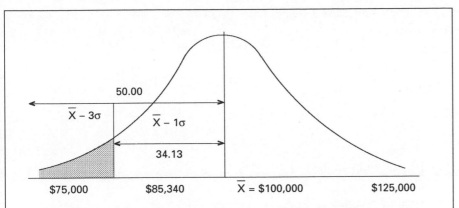

The shaded area under the curve is the probability that cash sales will be less than $85,340. The area shown by $\overline{X} - \sigma$ is 34.13; this is found from the table in Exhibit 4–13. If half the area is covered by the range $\overline{X} - 3\sigma$ to $\overline{X}$, then the shaded area must be the difference between 50.00 and 34.13, or 15.87. This is interpreted as the probability that cash sales will be less than $85,340. There is a 15.87 percent chance that cash sales will be lower than $85,340.

EXHIBIT 4–14 PROBABILITY OF CASH SALES LESS THAN $85,340

The ratio method assumes that cash flow is expected to vary directly with the level of another factor or:

$$CF = \beta_1 F_1$$

where:

β_1 is the ratio of CF to F_1

For example, if we know that 15 percent of each month's sales historically have been made for cash (letting the $\beta_1 = .15$), we forecast the future monthly sales level (F_1), say $100,000, to give us a forecast of the future month's cash flow:

$$CF = \$100,000 \times .15 = \$15,000$$

An example for disbursements may be that given a sales level in month t, the company normally replenishes inventory and pays for it in month t+1. Given a sales level of $100,000 for January, the company purchases and pays for inventory at a 60 percent level ($F = .6$); therefore the cash outflow in February is:

$$CF_{FEB} = Sales_{JAN} \times F_1$$

$$CF_{FEB} = \$100,000 \times .60$$

$$CF_{FEB} = \$60,000$$

The growth method can be used if the company expects cash flows to grow at a constant or variable rate over time.

$$CF_t = (1 + g)F_{t-1}$$

where:

CF_t is the cash flow in month t.

g is the growth rate.

F_{t-1} is the level of the factor in month $t - 1$.

Certain cash disbursements are expected to grow at 1 percent per month from the previous month's level of $100,000, then:

$$CF_t = (1 + .01)(100,000)$$

$$CF_t = \$101,000$$

The final forecasting method we will consider is one that involves the entire model; the cash flow depends upon more than one variable or factor. Experience has indicated to the forecaster that the cash outflow on a given day is 50 percent of the dollar amount of invoices (I) that were received 30 days earlier, plus 49 percent of the invoices received 35 days earlier. The cash outflow can be forecasted if we know that on day $t - 30$ we had received $50,000 of invoices and on day $t - 35$ we had received $60,000 of invoices.

$$
\begin{aligned}
CF_t &= \beta_1 F_1 + \beta_2 F_2 \\
&= \beta_1 I_{t-30} + \beta_2 I_{t-35} \\
&= .5(50,000) + .49(60,000) \\
CF_t &= \$54,400
\end{aligned}
$$

The next and final step in using any or all of these methods for forecasting is to determine the βs. Faced with the problem of forecasting anything, most people fall back on judgment and experience. Based on experience, the forecaster knows that customer Y always pays in 30 days, whereas customer Z always pays in 32 days. Given sales of $10,000 to Y and $15,000 to Z on the 1st of March, the forecaster can predict that on the 31st of March there will be a cash inflow of $10,000, and on the 2nd of April there will be a cash inflow of $15,000.

A more general approach to forecasting is time series analysis. Using the general model developed earlier we can form a time series model that seeks to forecast cash flow based on past observations (or experience) of cash flow. The model can be:

$$CF_{t+1} = \alpha + \beta_1 CF_t + \beta_2(F_{t-1}) + \ldots$$

where:

CF$_{t+1}$ is forecasted cash flow.

CF$_t$, CF$_{t-1}$ are the past levels of cash flow.

α, β_1, and β_2 are the coefficients that need to be estimated by the time series model.

For example, if there is a strong weekly cycle to cash flows, we might want to forecast next Wednesday's cash flow based on our experience with the previous three Wednesdays' cash flows, or:

$$CF_{next\ Wednesday} = \alpha + \beta_1\ CF_{last\ Wednesday} + \beta_2 CF_{2\ Wednesdays\ ago}$$

$$+ \beta_3 CF_{3\ Wednesdays\ ago}$$

The great advantage of using time series analysis is that it allows the forecaster to capture daily, seasonal, or cyclical patterns or trends that the company may be experiencing.

One technique that can be used to estimate the coefficients (βs) used in any or all of the models discussed above is *regression analysis*. As we have seen, we are interested in specifying the relationship between two variables (CF and F). We can refer to the cash flow (CF) as the dependent variable, and F as the independent variable. Because we cannot expect a perfect relationship between CF and F, we can write the relationship as:

$$CF = \alpha + \beta_1 F_1 + e$$

where:

e is a random error term.

The error occurs because we cannot measure F$_1$ with perfect accuracy and/or we don't know α and β_1 with perfect accuracy. Regression is a technique that mathematically fits a line to a series of points on a scatter diagram as shown in Exhibit 4–15.

Fitting a line to a series of points on a scatter diagram can be done in several ways. One method involves fitting a line by "eyeballing" the data. Clearly, this method will lead to arbitrarily drawn lines depending on individual preference. A more sophisticated technique, known as the "method of least squares," allows us to consistently determine a line according to an agreed upon set of criteria.

The method of least squares is a technique that fits a line by minimizing the sum of the squared error terms. The error terms (e) are the difference between the actual observed data and the regression line as shown in Exhibit 4–16.

As an example of the regression technique, consider a company whose monthly sales fluctuate between $500 and $1400 per month. The monthly cash disbursements vary between $160 and $400 per month. The historical data for the company is shown in Exhibit 4–17 in both tabular and scatter diagram form.

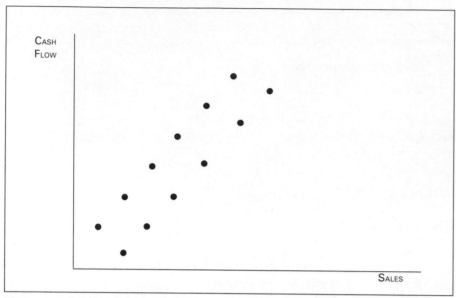

Exhibit 4–15   Scatter Diagram

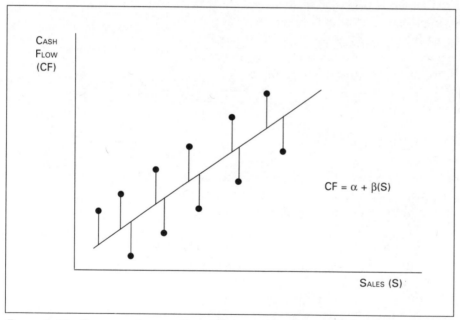

Exhibit 4–16   Regression Line and Error Terms

The issue at hand is whether we can establish a relationship between monthly cash outflows and monthly sales. "Eyeballing" the scatter diagram in Exhibit 4–17, we get the impression that as sales increase so do cash outflows. Alternatively, we can run a regression on the data using a spreadsheet program. The output of such a regression is presented in Exhibit 4–18.

From Exhibit 4–18 we can see that the regression equation for the relationship between cash outflow and sales is:

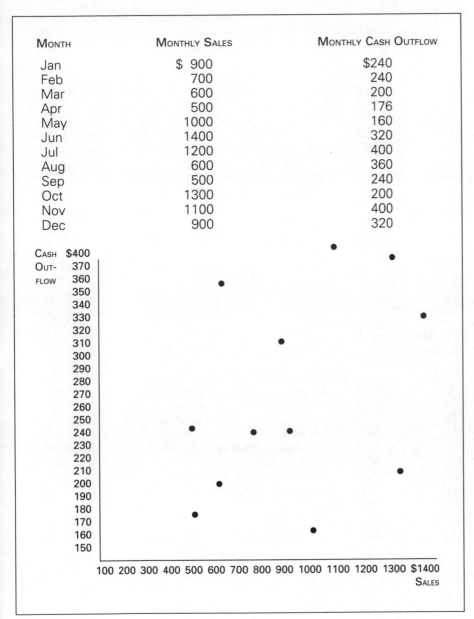

Month	Monthly Sales	Monthly Cash Outflow
Jan	$ 900	$240
Feb	700	240
Mar	600	200
Apr	500	176
May	1000	160
Jun	1400	320
Jul	1200	400
Aug	600	360
Sep	500	240
Oct	1300	200
Nov	1100	400
Dec	900	320

Exhibit 4–17   Sales and Cash Disbursements

$$CF_t = 551 + 1.25(S_t) + e$$

with:

$$\text{An } R^2 \text{ equal to .115999.}$$

This model shows that if we want to forecast monthly cash outflows, we can use a forecast of monthly sales multiplied by 1.25 and add 551. This will give us an estimate of the monthly cash outflow. However, we are also interested in how accurate or how good this forecast is. The R^2 of 11.6 percent can be interpreted to solve this. An R^2 of 11.6 percent indicates

	MONTHLY SALES		MONTHLY CASH FLOWS			
Jan	$ 900	Jan	$240			
Feb	700	Feb	240			
Mar	600	Mar	200			
Apr	500	Apr	176		Regression Output:	
May	1000	May	160	Constant		551.3513
Jun	1400	Jun	320	Standard error of Y estimate		310.2939
Jul	1200	Jul	400	R squared		0.115999
Aug	600	Aug	360	Number of observations		12
Sep	500	Sep	240	Degrees of freedom		10
Oct	1300	Oct	200			
Nov	1100	Nov	400	X coefficient(s)		1.254233
Dec	900	Dec	320	Standard error of coefficient(s)		1.094903

EXHIBIT 4–18   REGRESSION OUTPUT FOR SALES AND CASH OUTFLOWS

	MONTHLY SALES		MONTHLY CASH FLOWS			
Jan	$ 900					
Feb	700	Feb	$240			
Mar	600	Mar	200			
Apr	500	Apr	176		Regression Output:	
May	1000	May	160	Constant		−86.9456
Jun	1400	Jun	320	Standard error of Y estimate		94.95514
Jul	1200	Jul	400	R squared		0.925489
Aug	600	Aug	360	Number of observations		11
Sep	500	Sep	240	Degrees of freedom		9
Oct	1300	Oct	200			
Nov	1100	Nov	400	X coefficient(s)		.3566446
Dec	900	Dec	320	Standard error of coefficient(s)		.0337315

EXHIBIT 4–19   REGRESSION OUTPUT FOR CASH OUTFLOWS LAGGED ONE MONTH

that the variation in monthly sales explains 11.6 percent of the variation in monthly cash outflows. The other 88.4 percent of variation in cash outflows is explained by random factors denoted by the "e" in the regression equation. This is not very good for forecasting purposes, so we might want to look at the information in a slightly different fashion. For example, if we know that all inventory is purchased and paid for in the month after the sale, we might want to see if there is a lagged relationship between cash outflows in month t +1 and in month t. Exhibit 4–19 contains the regression information for this case.

We can see from the high R^2 of 92.5 percent that the level of sales in month t is a very good explanator of the level of cash flow in month t +1. The forecasting equation in this case is:

$$CF_{t+1} = -86.9 + .356(sales_t) + e$$

We now have a method for estimating the coefficients or relationship between various factors and cash flow. We also have a way of measuring how good the established relationship is. That is, we can look at the R^2. The range of values for R^2 is from 0 to 100 percent, with 0 indicating no explanatory power and 100 percent indicating perfect explanatory power.

Linear regression can assist the forecaster in making reasonable estimates of future cash flows. However, a word of caution is necessary at this point. A straight line can be fitted to any set of data even if there is no linear relationship underlying the data; therefore, we must use the R^2 to see how well the regression line fits the data. Another problem involves the nature of the underlying relationship. Just because cash flow is linked to the previous month's sales during one year does not mean that this will always be so. If, for instance, the company changes its inventory and/or payments policy, the relationship between sales and cash flow will also change. The analysts must be aware of changes in the company's policies and keep their forecasting models current to reflect actual conditions.

➤ SUMMARY

Cash flow forecasting can be classified by duration or time period of forecast (long, medium, and short) and approach (receipts and disbursements and adjusted net income). The basic purpose of forecasting cash flow is to provide information to the cash manager so that he or she can formulate a plan for managing the cash flow.

Forecasting is both an art and a science. The art portion is related to the forecaster's ability to use personal judgment based on his or her experience when making a forecast. The science part is related to using statistical techniques such as linear regression in uncovering relationships between various types of information. A good forecast relies on both.

CHAPTER 5

CASH MOBILIZATION TECHNIQUES

By the end of this chapter, the reader will be able to:

LEARNING OBJECTIVES

1. Differentiate between cash collection and disbursement techniques.
2. Develop a cash gathering procedure.
3. Describe three types of float.
4. Explain five cash collection techniques.
5. Devise a cash concentration system.

Cash mobilization means freeing up unused or underused corporate cash. We have seen how a company's working capital moves from cash to inventory to accounts receivable and back into cash. We have also seen how cash is used to pay bills or reduce accounts payable. If a company does not collect its receivables as quickly as possible or if it pays its bills sooner than necessary, it needlessly reduces the amount of cash at its disposal. Cash mobilization techniques locate these hidden sources of cash and make them available for company use. The two principles of cash mobilization have historically been to speed up cash gathering and to slow down cash disbursement. However, the cash manager of the 1990s focuses on cash synchronization and controlled cash disbursement. Given the breakthroughs in electronic cash and information movement technology, this area is assured of many changes in the next decade.

➤ CASH GATHERING

Cash gathering refers to the complete sequence of steps that a company takes to receive usable cash from its customers. Usable cash refers to money the company can spend. Simply receiving a check from a customer does not create usable cash because this check must be deposited in the company's checking account and must usually be cleared by the customer's bank.

A cash manager has many opportunities to speed up cash gathering throughout the billing and receiving operation. Each of the steps in this operation should be examined individually to see if it can be eliminated or done more quickly and efficiently. The steps are:

1. Company prepares bill for customer.
2. Company mails bill.
3. Bill arrives at customer's location.
4. Customer reviews bill and mails check.
5. Check arrives at company office.
6. Company reviews check and deposits it.
7. Check clears through customer's bank account.
8. Cash is available for company use.

By reviewing this detailed list of collection steps, we can begin to see where bottlenecks occur and what to do about them.

Prompt Billing

Beginning with the first step, an obvious but often overlooked way to accelerate cash inflow is to get the bills to customers faster. For example, if Company A bills monthly with 30-day credit terms, its customers will begin counting their 30 days on receipt of the bill. Suppose Company A converts to twice-monthly billing. Now, customers who still comply with the 30-day credit terms will send checks sooner. Company A might also move to weekly billing or, in the ultimate case, to billing with each day's orders. In this case, Company A could even include the invoice with the shipped materials, eliminating any delay between receipt of goods and receipt of bill by the customer.

A shorter billing cycle is certainly attractive for speeding up cash inflow, but not all companies can reduce their billing cycles. There are several reasons for this:

1. The paperwork involved in preparing bills more often than monthly may not justify the faster cash inflow.
2. Customers who are used to monthly billing may ignore bills received in the middle of the month and therefore not pay any faster. (This is particularly true when a company sends many bills during the month and a summary statement at the end of the month.)
3. Credit is a competitive marketing tool, and the competitive situation may not allow a shorter billing cycle (which effectively reduces credit).
4. The small dollar value of each transaction may not justify billing more often than monthly.
5. The nature of the business (particularly service businesses) may not logically lend itself to billing more often than monthly.

Even companies that can bill only monthly find it worthwhile to make sure that billing information flows quickly to the accounting department. For example, if billing information typically takes three days to travel to accounting, then when bills are prepared at the end of the month, the last three days of sales for the month will not be billed until the following month. By reducing the time for billing information to flow to accounting by two days, this company can add the extra two days of billing to each month's invoices.

Of all the steps in collecting money from customers, the company has least control over when the customer reviews the bill and mails the check. However, a company can take several actions to encourage customers to pay quickly. The first is to submit an accurate and easy-to-understand bill. Accuracy is important because, if the customer finds an error, valuable time will be lost while the error is corrected. Bills should be easy to understand so that they may be processed quickly. Complicated bills cause misunderstandings (which can take just as much time to correct as actual errors) or delays in processing, during which time customers are paying their simpler bills.

A company can also affect the promptness of customer payments by the terms it offers. Offering a cash discount of 1 or 2 percent for payment within ten days will encourage many customers to pay quickly. Before a company offers a cash discount, it must consider several things:

1. The average time customers will take to pay without a discount (which is usually not 30 days but, more typically, 40 or 50 days).
2. The speed with which customers will pay 10-day discount invoices. (Even here, customers may take more than 10 days and still deduct the discount.)
3. The percentage of customers who will take advantage of a discount.
4. The benefit of having extra cash compared to the cost of the discounts.

Instead of offering a discount for prompt payment, some companies charge a penalty for late payment, typically 1.5 percent interest per month on the unpaid balance. This is most commonly done with consumer accounts and only occasionally with business accounts. Charging interest is subject to strict federal laws and additional state laws that vary widely from one state to another. When used with business accounts, late payment penalties may cause ill will and can be difficult to collect.

Companies can also speed up collections by making it easy for customers to pay. A common technique is to enclose a preaddressed envelope or even a postage-paid envelope. Companies use this technique more often with consumer accounts, but in any case it should be tested carefully to make sure that the faster collections more than pay the extra cost of envelopes and postage.

Finally, companies should stay in close contact with all overdue accounts. The accounting department should age all accounts receivable by showing the total dollar value of accounts outstanding for less than 30 days, 30 to 60 days, 60 to 90 days, and so on. By comparing this report with earlier reports, the financial manager can tell if receivables are too high by historical standards. Furthermore, all overdue accounts should be contacted directly by mail or phone. If customers with delinquent accounts are called regularly, they will pay your bills before they pay someone else's because they know your concern and they would like you to stop calling.

DECENTRALIZED RECEIVABLES

The simplest way to receive payments is to instruct customers to send their checks to company headquarters. The accounting office then compares the check with the original invoice and deposits it. However, this procedure requires time for the check to arrive in the mail, time for the accounting office to review and deposit the check, and time for the check to clear the customer's bank.

If customers are scattered throughout the country, checks from these customers take many days to arrive at company headquarters; during this time, the money is not available for company use. To speed up collections, companies decentralize their receivables collection procedures and collect customer checks at several places around the country. This significantly reduces the mailing time of customer checks.

The most commonly used collection centers are the company's branch locations, which are in various cities. Someone from the branch office then deposits the checks in a nearby bank. Because the bank is near the customers, the checks clear quickly, and the money is then available for company use.

In many companies, local bank balances build up and are then forwarded (by check or some other transfer device) to the disbursing account at headquarters. This system has several disadvantages. First, the local branch office may not be in an optimum location for fast funds transfers. The office is probably close to customers, but it may not be in a Federal Reserve city, thus slowing the transfer of funds to headquarters. Second, any delay in processing customer checks in the branch office will slow down the movement of funds to the home office.

> ## Cash Collection, Disbursement, and Concentration Systems

The efficiency of a cash management system depends on the synchronization of cash inflows and outflows. So far as cash inflows exceed cash outflows, the firm will have a surplus of funds and will need to invest in appropriate money market instruments. Obviously, if a firm has a net cash outflow, it will have to borrow funds to meet its financial obligations. Many firms employ sophisticated cash concentration systems where money is moved from many small accounts into one or several large master accounts. This facilitates control and efficiency. In addition, many firms utilize electronic funds transfers to reduce costly delays of incoming receipts. Alternatively, some firms use remote or "controlled" disbursement sites, hoping to delay outgoing funds.

Although cash management objectives in the past may have been to speed up inflows and slow down outflows, the current goal of most cash managers is to improve the cash synchronization of incoming receipts and disbursements. Much has happened to cash management in the last decade to improve the flow of funds and information. In the following section, we provide an overview of some of the more important developments.

> ## Cash Collection
> ## Systems

Generally, the level of sophistication of a cash collection system depends on the type of receipts received by an organization and the geographical dispersion of corporate branches and subsidiaries. Some common characteristics that all cash collection systems should provide are funds mobilization, accurate accounts receivable data, and access to reliable information. The need for reliable information should be clear. Cash managers need to be constantly updated on cash inflows and outflows and bank balances so that they can properly invest surplus funds or cover deficits. In addition, accurate accounts receivable information is necessary to ensure that customers are paying balances promptly and are receiving commensurate credit. A breakdown of accounts receivable information could create losses to the firm or a loss of customer goodwill.

The purpose of funds mobilization is to move funds from the payor to the firm's banking network as efficiently and economically as possible. The immediate goal of a cash mobilization network is to reduce costly float. There are basically three types of float: mail, processing, and transit. *Mail float* is the time lapse between the moment a customer mails a check and the moment the selling firm begins to process it. The range of this float is usually from zero to five days for domestic payments; this may be much longer for foreign transactions. *Processing float* is the time it takes the selling firm to deposit a check into the bank after receiving it. This may range from zero to three calendar days. *Transit float*, or *availability float*, is the time required for a check to clear through the banking system and become a usable source of funds for the firm. Checks are processed through either the Federal Reserve system or a local clearing house. Checks cleared through the Federal Reserve system require a maximum of two days but only one day if the paying bank and the collecting bank are in the same Federal Reserve district. (There are 12 districts.) Availability float ranges from zero to five days. This is the time when the bank makes the funds available for corporate use. It is not necessarily the time it takes for the check to clear through the clearing house network. Exhibit 5–1 illustrates the three types of float.

Float is measured by the time lag and the dollars involved. The calculation of the two measures multiplied together is referred to as *dollar–days float*. For example, suppose a customer in Boston mails a check to a supplier in New York on Monday. The check will probably arrive at the supplier's office on Wednesday and, most likely, will be forwarded to the supplier's New York bank on Wednesday or Thursday. In this instance, the supplier will have collected the funds by Thursday or Friday. Now take a similar situation in which the only difference is that the customer is located in Denver, Colorado. At least two additional days can probably be added to the mailing time, and an additional two days will elapse before the company's bank will consider the proceeds collected and therefore usable by its customer, the supplier.

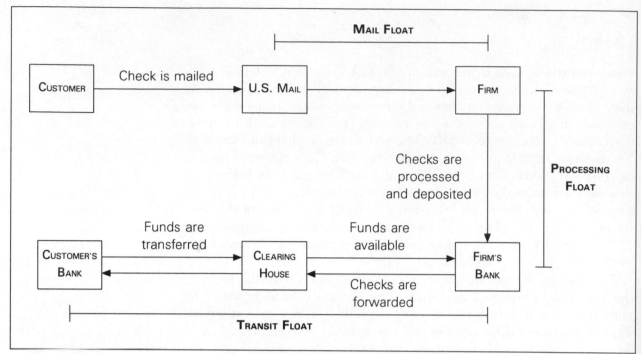

Exhibit 5–1   Types of Float

If an average day's collection is $200,000 and if a company's cost of debt is 10 percent, the dollar–days float is equal to $400,000 (2 × $200,000). The annual interest lost due to funds unavailable for investment or the interest paid because of funds tied up in mail float is equal to $40,000. This is the product of the reduced float multiplied by the opportunity cost of funds ($400,000 × 10 percent). The cost of float is usually compared to the cost of cash collection techniques. If the cost of implementing a new technique is less than the cost of the float, the firm will choose to introduce the new technique. Some examples of cash collection techniques include lockboxes, preauthorized payments, depository transfer checks, and wire transfers. These and other cash collection techniques are explained below.

A *lockbox* is a separate depository account into which incoming checks are deposited (see Exhibit 5–2). Customers mail payments directly to a post office box that is monitored by a bank or a third party. The bank or third party will pick up the mail at the central post office (as often as 20 times a day) and deliver the checks to the processing facility. At the processing center the envelopes are opened and the checks are removed and encoded. The check amounts are compared to the return documents, recorded, and entered into the clearing process. Envelopes, photocopies of the checks, and all other mail sent to the lockbox are forwarded by the bank to its customer. In many instances, the bank makes funds available one day after the check is received. However, the availability of funds is a function of the following elements: the Federal Reserve clearing times, average clearing time of different cities (Phoenix-Hecht publishes data on this), and bank-by-bank availability.

LOCKBOXES

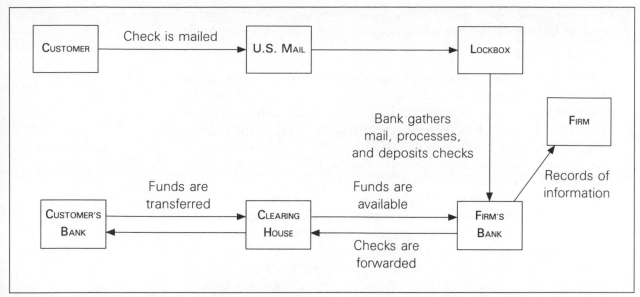

EXHIBIT 5–2   THE LOCKBOX SYSTEM

Before a firm engages in a lockbox arrangement it will often subscribe to a mail time survey by an independent consultant. Phoenix-Hecht, for example, reports mail times between central city post offices. The eventual location of a lockbox will depend on several factors. For example, a lockbox located in the Federal Reserve or a Regional Check Processing Center (RCPC) usually receives faster availability than a lockbox that is located elsewhere. In addition, many firms like to select a lockbox that is close to a hub airport. Obviously, this may reduce valuable mail float. Finally, the selection of lockbox sites must account for the geographical concentration of the customer base and volume. The ideal lockbox will be strategically located between the customers and the central bank. As an example of assessing the costs and benefits of a lockbox plan, assume that the JMS Corporation is considering the adoption of a lockbox system. At present, it takes six days for customers' payments to reach the company and an additional two days before the deposits are made. The firm now has an average daily cash collection of $700,000, and the lockbox system would reduce the total billing and processing time to two and one-half days. In addition, assume that the annual costs for the lockbox are $150,000.

The reduction in cash balances with the new system is equal to (6 + 2 − 2.5 days) × ($700,000), or a total of $3,850,000. If the company is able to invest short-term funds at 7 percent, the adoption of the system results in additional income of $269,500 (.07 × $3,850,000) from the additional funds made available. Since the cost of the new system is $150,000, the plan should be introduced given that the benefits exceed the costs of $119,500 ($269,500 − $150,000).

Both banks and large firms that have many offices often use transfer techniques for moving funds between banks. The most popular transfer tech-

OTHER CASH COLLECTION TECHNIQUES

niques include depository transfer checks, electronic depository transfer checks, wire transfers, preauthorized checks, direct sends, and sweep accounts.

1. *Depository transfer checks (DTCs)* are preprinted, nonnegotiable instruments payable only to the bank of deposit (the regional or central/concentration bank). Customer checks are processed and deposited in local banks used by the subsidiaries or divisions, and a DTC is mailed to the firm's concentration bank. The local bank processes the checks and transfers the funds to the concentration bank while the DTC is in the mail. The corporate account will have the use of the funds once the DTC has been received and cleared. This usually takes several days.

2. *Electronic depository transfer checks* clear in one day. An electronic DTC may cost less than an ordinary DTC and avoids the uncertainty associated with mailing. Deposit information is transferred from the firm to the concentration bank several times during the day. The concentration bank then completes a DTC and credits it to the firm's account. An electronic DTC is then sent to the firm's local bank requesting funds.

3. *Wire transfers* are another means of transferring funds between banks. Wire transfers may be sent through a bank wire system or the Federal Reserve system. In either case, funds are made available on the same day. The cost, however, is quite high compared with other transfer techniques. Cash managers need to consider the tradeoff between decreasing float and increasing transfer costs. Wire transfers are generally suitable only for transferring large amounts on a periodic basis.

4. *Preauthorized checks* are sometimes used by firms that receive a large number of regular payments. A preauthorized check appears to be an ordinary check, but it does not require the signature of the person on whose account it is being drawn. Thus, the customer authorizes the firm to draw checks directly from the customer's demand deposit account. This procedure reduces mail and processing float and ensures consistency and certainty of payment.

5. *Direct sends* are used by corporations to reduce transit float. Corporations that receive large checks drawn on banks in distant cities, or a large number of checks drawn on banks in a particular city, may arrange to present these checks directly to the banks on which they are drawn. Direct sends enable the firm to receive immediate payment thereby avoiding the delay associated with the clearing process.

6. *Sweep accounts* allow a corporation to drop the balance in its checking account to a minimum balance at the end of each day. Funds that are freed up by "sweeping the account" are then transferred to a centralized disbursement account or invested overnight to earn interest income.

➤ Cash Disbursement Systems

The primary purpose of a disbursement system is to minimize the net cost of delivering payments to a company's employees, suppliers, and stockholders. Some of the principal costs include opportunity cost from investments not made or interest expense from unnecessary borrowings; transfer costs associated with moving funds from one location to another; costs associated with lost discounts, or opportunity costs of late or early payments; costs associated with vendor or employee ill will; managerial costs of handling the disbursement system; and costs of having unauthorized disbursements.

Opportunity cost can be reduced by using a system that increases disbursement float (the time elapsed from when a check is mailed until it actually clears). This can be accomplished by mailing checks from a remote disbursement location. However, corporate managers need to recognize that another objective of a cash management system is to maintain strong relationships with vendors. Intentionally late payments or exaggerated mail float might create ill will among vendors and employees and cause the firm problems in the future.

Many cash managers are concerned about inefficiencies and lack of control in cash disbursements and attempt to minimize excess account balances whenever possible. The following cash-disbursement techniques are designed to improve control over payments and increase the amount of float.

Zero Balance Accounts

Zero balance accounts (ZBAs) provide centralized cash control at the main corporate office. The ZBA is a specialized disbursement account in which checks are written on an account with a zero balance. A ZBA system requires all accounts to be included in the same concentration bank. Authorized employees are still able to write checks on their individual accounts, but no funds will be maintained in these accounts. Divisional employees write checks and accumulate a negative bank balance daily. At the end of each day the daily negative balance is cleared by the release of funds from a corporate master account. Consequently, at the end of each day the divisional bank balances are restored to zero. The zero balance account offers the firm with many operating divisions several benefits:

- Greater centralized control over disbursements.
- Elimination of redundant idle bank balances.
- Reduction of cash transfer expenses.
- More effective cash investments.
- Greater autonomy for local managers.

Payable Through Drafts

Payable through drafts are similar to checks in that they are a written order to pay and have the physical appearance of checks. However, they are not drawn on a bank. Rather, drafts are drawn on and authorized by the issuing firm and presented to the issuing firm's bank. After the bank receives a draft, it sends the draft back to the issuing firm and awaits approval. Funds are not released until the corporate issuer has approved those drafts that he or she wishes to pay. The bank will generally withhold payment for one business day and will then cover the payment automatically unless directed otherwise. The issuing firm generally inspects the drafts for inaccuracies in signatures, amounts, and dates. Payments on issued drafts can be canceled easily if any discrepancies are found.

Although drafts may give the firm extra float time, their main advantage lies in ensuring effective control over field payments. Draft payments are popular in the insurance industry, for instance, where field agents are able to settle claims quickly even though they lack the authority to issue checks. By using drafts, the central office improves efficiency in field operations yet still exercises the option to eliminate any payments deemed inappropriate.

Exhibit 5–3 shows a summary of cash collection and disbursement techniques.

➤ CASH CONCENTRATION
SYSTEMS

A cash concentration system is designed to move funds from many small accounts into one or several large master accounts as efficiently as possible. Exhibit 5–4 illustrates an example. A cash concentration network improves the control of the cash manager. By having a cash concentration system, the cash manager can devote considerable time to managing the balances of one large account. Forecasting total cash flows for the master account may result in a smaller percentage of error than that associated with estimating cash balances of many small accounts. In addition, the cash manager is able to invest these funds at higher rates, since pooling funds enables the cash manager to buy larger blocks of investment securities or money market instruments that are sold in large dollar denominations. Finally, the cash concentration network helps reduce the excess balances existing in many of the company's smaller banks and the transfer expenses of disbursing funds.

The use of DTCs, wire transfers, and lockboxes is intended to improve the efficiency of the firm's cash flows and investments. The type of system that a firm employs will depend on the average dollar volume of its transactions, the number and sophistication of its banks, the timing and type of information it requires, and the current opportunity cost of float. For example, DTCs are preferable to wire transfers if the dollar amounts of the funds being transferred are low and the volume of transactions is high since DTCs are much less expensive than wire transfers. However, if the transaction volume is very high and disbursements are known ahead of time (such as payroll), the firm might utilize an Automated Clearing House (ACH) transfer. An ACH transaction is often used for high-volume transactions and regular (or batch) transactions. A bank prepares an ACH magnetic tape detailing all the necessary information regarding payors and payees, amounts, and so on and then sends it to the Automated Clearing House. Availability for this transaction is usually one day. Though the availability is not immediate, as it would be for a wire transfer, it is slightly less expensive than a DTC and may serve a useful purpose when handling certain types of payments.

The trend of cash concentration systems is to improve on float management and information. For example, ACH tapes can now be deposited on

TECHNIQUE	PURPOSE	DESCRIPTION
CASH COLLECTION		
Lockbox	Reduces mail, processing, and transit float	A separate depository account that permits the firm's bank to collect and process receipts
Depository transfer check	Promotes efficient utilization of funds	A preprinted, nonnegotiable check that transfers funds between banks
Electronic depository transfer check	Reduces the mail float of a DTC	A means of transmitting deposit information electronically to a bank
Wire transfer	Eliminates mail, processing, and transit float	A vehicle for transferring funds between banks immediately
Preauthorized check	Reduces processing and mail float	A check written by the firm and drawn on the customer's account that by mutual agreement does not require the customer's signature
Direct send	Reduces transit float	An arrangement for presenting checks directly to banks on which they are drawn
Sweep account	Promotes efficient utilization of funds	A technique to drop the checking account balance to a minimum level at the end of each day
CASH DISBURSEMENT		
Zero balance accounts	Increase the efficient use of cash payments, cash balances, and float	Checks are drawn on accounts in a concentration banking network, and the balance of each account is restored to $0 on a daily basis
Controlled disbursement	Increases positive float	Checks are issued from banks that are geographically distant from the receiver
Draft	Increases control over payments and increases positive float	Drafts require an approval from the firm prior to release of funds

EXHIBIT 5-3   SUMMARY OF CASH COLLECTION AND DISBURSEMENT TECHNIQUES

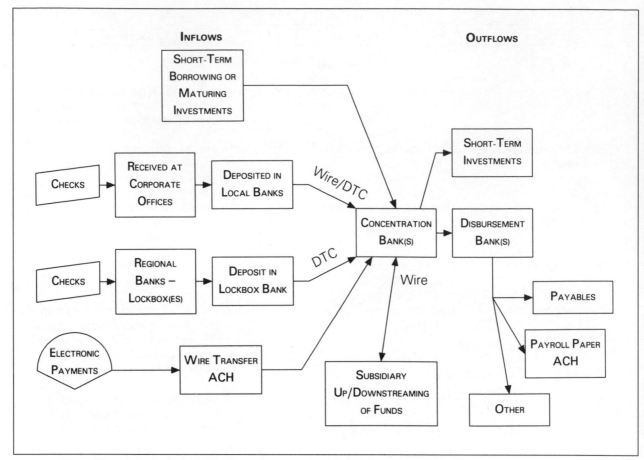

Exhibit 5–4   A Typical Concentration System

weekends to help reduce the firm's risk of an overdraft. Future cash concentration systems should continue to make strides in reducing excess balances, administrative costs, and transfer costs and should be better able to provide the cash manager with reliable information for purposes of investing funds and preparing appropriate lines of credit.

➢ Automated Clearing Houses

ACH is an acronym for the automated clearing house, an electronic computer-based system for making payments. ACH is an electronic payment and receipt service used for recurring payments and receipts to and from accounts at depository institutions. For example, the U.S. government uses ACH for its military and civilian payrolls and Social Security benefits.

The money management uses of ACH are attractive to large companies and consist of two applications: bill collection and cash concentration. Unlike payments made by check, the ACH transactions may be originated by the payee, who takes the money out of the payor's account when preauthorized by the payor to do so. For example, a utility consumer can pre-authorize the electric company to use ACH to originate payment to pay the consumer's utility bill.

Usually, two ACH entries result from every ACH transaction. An entry is made putting money into the account of the payee, and another entry is made taking money out of the account of the payor. Each ACH entry has an accompanying description. The two most common ones are prearranged payment and deposit (PPD) and cash concentration or disbursement (CCD). An example of a PPD is a mortgage payment made through ACH. The homeowner authorizes his bank to permit automatic payment from his bank account on a certain day each month for the mortgage payment. Another example of a PPD would be the direct deposit of payroll checks.

As an example of a CCD, cash concentration, we can think of a chain of retail outlets. At the end of each business day, each store deposits cash from its daily sales receipts at a local bank. The central management of the retail chain can then concentrate the cash in a bank in order to invest in short-term money market instruments the next morning.

➤ Cash Control

All forms of control are important to a company. Cash control is especially important because errors can lead to overdrawn accounts, loss of supplier discounts, and loss of investment opportunities. Cash managers control cash in several ways; bank balance versus book balance, use of computers, separate accounts, and intercompany cash balances.

Bank Balance Versus Book Balance

The company's books show a cash balance different from the bank's books. These differences arise from uncollected deposits (deposited checks that have not yet cleared through the customer's account) and from float (checks written by the company but not yet presented for payment). Uncollected deposits make the company's cash balance (shown on company books) appear larger than it really is; on the other hand, float makes the actual cash balance in the bank larger than shown on the company books. Companies must carefully monitor these two differing amounts to know their actual cash balance at any time. Companies that play the float must monitor the actual balance precisely at all times, but all companies must keep track of their bank balances to avoid writing bad checks.

Use of Computers in Receivables and Payables

All companies should age their accounts receivable; that is, they should calculate the total dollar volume of receivables outstanding for 30 days, 60 days, and so on. If a company uses a computer to prepare invoices, simple programs make it possible to age accounts receivable automatically.

Computers can also help with accounts payable. Companies can now enter into a computer all bills when they arrive in the mail. The computer can then produce payment checks on a daily, weekly, or monthly basis—automatically taking advantage of all desired supplier discounts—and write checks for other bills at the latest acceptable date. Furthermore, because the computer contains all bills and their planned payment dates, the machine can print out the company's cash needs for the coming one to two months, which helps with short-term cash forecasting.

Companies often maintain separate accounts for different purposes in order to maintain cash control. For example, a company may maintain separate accounts for receipts, accounts payable, payroll, dividends, and investments. Companies usually maintain all these accounts at the same bank. The company writes all its payroll checks on the payroll account. On the day it distributes these checks to employees, it also transfers enough money from the main disbursing account to cover all the payroll checks. Separate accounts help a company see more clearly where its cash is going.

Separate Accounts

   Multiple accounts present two problems. First, if the company maintains a balance in each account, the sum of these balances may be greater than the amount of cash that would be required in a single account. Second, the company must carefully monitor interaccount transfers in order to keep track of its exact cash balance in each account. Otherwise, the company may find that a transfer is temporarily lost, and the books will show less cash than is actually available; or transferred money may show up in two accounts, and the amount of cash available will then be overstated.

Many companies today have decentralized their operations and have established a number of profit centers. These same companies, however, usually maintain tight central control over cash management. The advantages of centralized cash management include simpler bank relations, concentrated borrowing power, a single set of investment policies and procedures, and the elimination of cash imbalances (which might cause one division to borrow money at 10 percent while another division was investing money at 6 percent).

Intercompany Cash Balances

➤ Summary

In this chapter, we saw how companies improve their cash collection and disbursement systems. Companies can accelerate cash collections by preparing bills quickly, employing DTCs, using wire transfers, or implementing preauthorized checks. Alternatively, companies may utilize drafts, controlled disbursements, or zero balance accounts to improve the distribution of cash payments. Cash managers of the 1990s will be utilizing electronic funds transfers more often and will need to be well versed in the latest finance and computer technology. Many changes have occurred in the area of cash mobilization in the last decade, and many more are expected in the next.

CHAPTER 6

BANK SERVICES, CHARGES, AND RELATIONS

By the end of this chapter, the reader will be able to:

1. Describe the various services offered by commercial banks.
2. Differentiate between the various methods of compensating banks for their services.
3. Enumerate the criteria used in selecting a commercial bank.
4. Describe the criteria used by companies in evaluating their banks.

Banks play an important part in any cash management program. For a cash manager to make the most effective use of banks, he or she should understand the many services they offer and the costs of these services. In this chapter, we first discuss the impact of cash management programs on banks. Banks are both helped and hurt by the increasing number of corporate cash management programs. Banks are hurt because an effective cash management program reduces the levels of cash in the company's demand accounts. At the same time, however, banks are helped because they can sell a wide variety of new services to companies with corporate cash management programs.

We next look closely at bank services. Banks no longer simply provide checking accounts and loans, but today they provide collection services to include: lockboxes, preauthorized checks and electronic debits, and precoded deposits; disbursement services to include remote-controlled disbursements, zero balance accounts, and electronic payments; concentration services to include wire transfers, depository transfer checks, and electronic depository transfers; control services to include information reporting services, lockbox transmission, and pooling services. We then examine the costs of these services, in terms of either direct fees or compensating balance requirements.

Today, a cash manager has a wide variety of banks, services, and prices to choose from. We, therefore, discuss later in the chapter the criteria a cash manager may use in selecting banks.

Once a company has selected one or more banks, continuing communication is important, so we outline the principles involved in maintaining close contact with the bank officers. Finally, at the end of the chapter, we discuss the importance and methods of evaluating bank performance.

➣ IMPACT OF CASH MANAGEMENT PROGRAMS ON BANKS

The growing trend toward cash management affects banks in several ways. When a company collects its receivables faster and pays its bills more slowly, its bank gains because the company's cash balances are larger. If a company uses automatic wire transfers, the banks that receive the cash are helped, and those that lose deposits are hurt. When a company begins to monitor its cash balances and invest excess funds in attractive, short-term, outside opportunities (such as treasury bills or commercial paper), the average balance in the company's demand account is reduced, and this decreases the bank's lendable supply of interest-free money.

The net effect of a cash management program is usually to reduce the average balance a company maintains in its demand account. At first, many banks felt threatened by this reduction in deposits because banks lend these deposits; thus, a reduction leaves them with less money to lend. Then some banks realized that the scarcity of cash and the variety of attractive investment opportunities make corporate cash management programs inevitable. Rather than fight cash management programs, some banks developed new services to help cash managers. Other banks followed suit for competitive reasons. Today, banks work actively with their customers to help design more efficient cash gathering and disbursing systems. In this way, these banks have strengthened the relationship with their customers and have been able to sell a variety of new cash management services, such as lockboxes and accounts payable management.

➣ BANK SERVICES

Traditionally, banks provided checking accounts, savings accounts, and loans. They still provide these services, but they have greatly expanded their offerings. We look first at traditional bank services and then at the expanded offerings.

CHECKING ACCOUNTS

Banks still largely depend on demand deposits in checking accounts for money to lend to other customers. In addition to regular checking accounts, some banks also offer zero balance accounts (usually in conjunction with a company's main disbursing account). Zero balance accounts are specialized disbursement accounts on which checks are written even though the balances in the accounts are maintained at zero. Checks debited to a zero balance account for payment are covered by a transfer of funds from a master account in the firm's concentration bank. These accounts allow a company to control more closely the cash it uses for various purposes (branch offices, payrolls, and dividends) without necessarily tying up cash.

Banks have also developed interest-bearing checking accounts. These are called NOW accounts and are available only to individuals. If interest-paying checking accounts become widely available for businesses, cash managers will not have to worry quite so much about squeezing every last dollar out of the company checking account. On the other hand, since NOW accounts are becoming popular, banks will have to pay interest on money they formerly got free, and will, therefore, have to increase prices on other bank services.

Banks may not pay corporate customers interest on their demand deposits, but they may compensate the firm by giving earnings credits, provided that such credits are used by the company to compensate the bank for services rendered. Each bank has its own method of calculating earnings credits, but basically it is some predetermined rate multiplied by the company's available balances. The earnings credit rate is often tied to conditions in the money markets by being set as a function of the T-bill rate or some other short-term interest rate.

Although it varies from bank to bank, some banks allow monthly excess or deficit earnings credits to be accrued to future months, thereby allowing for one month's deficit to average out against another month's surplus. Over time, usually one year, any accumulated deficits will have to be made up by a cash payment and any accumulated surpluses will be lost.

SAVINGS ACCOUNTS

Most banks offer savings accounts for individuals, but many banks cannot by state law pay interest on savings accounts to corporations. Instead, some of these banks offer time deposit certificates, which are interest-bearing deposits with a fixed maturity date. Federal and state banking authorities regulate the rates and maturities, and in recent years, these rates have been lower than competing short-term investments. The liquidity of time deposit certificates is low because they are nonnegotiable (payable only to the original depositor) and have a fixed maturity date.

Many large banks also offer negotiable certificates of deposit (CDs), which are interest-bearing obligations of the bank. Because CDs are negotiable and because some banks and many government security dealers maintain an active secondary market for them, the CDs of major banks are quite liquid. Interest rates are generally competitive with other short-term investments.

LOANS

Banks today offer short-term (often 90-day) as well as long-term (1-year to 20-year) loans for real estate, buildings, and equipment. In addition, many banks lease equipment to large customers. Leases are a form of loan and are covered more fully in Chapter 8.

Cash managers typically use short-term loans from banks to cover peak seasonal needs for money. For example, a company may have to build up its inventory right before the peak selling season, and this increase in inventory ties up the company's cash. A short-term bank loan gives the company the cash it needs during this peak season. Similarly, if a company's customers traditionally stretch out the time they take to pay bills at a certain season (perhaps during the summer), a short-term bank loan can help the company finance these extra receivables and still maintain an adequate cash level.

In addition to making loans, banks offer lines of credit. A line of credit is an agreement by the bank to lend up to a certain amount of money, *if needed*, for a certain period of time. (We discuss lines of credit further in Chapter 7.) For example, a company may foresee that it could need as much as $500,000 next summer. Rather than wait until the last minute to arrange for this loan, the company may negotiate a line of credit. The bank then agrees to lend up to $500,000 on an as-needed basis. This assures the company that money will be available when needed but does not obligate the company to borrow the money. By extending a line of credit, the bank benefits in two ways. First, the agreement strengthens the bank's relationship with the customer and practically guarantees that the company will come to the bank when it needs money. Second, the bank often charges the company in some way (by a compensating balance requirement or a commitment fee) for extending a line of credit.

LINES OF CREDIT

Today, banks offer an increasing variety of financial advice and information. Analyses and advice include analysis of collection systems, analysis of funds concentration methods, recommended programs to reduce mail float and check collection float, investment advice, and analysis of disbursement systems. Banks also provide information to corporate customers. Such information includes collection reports, often by wire, from geographically scattered lockboxes; account reconciliation, often including float analysis; demand account monitoring and reporting, which include a daily report of account activity and the company's exact cash balance; foreign exchange rates; and quotes on selected money market instruments, including certificates of deposit, government and federal agency securities, commercial paper, and the Dow Jones industrial average.

FINANCIAL ADVICE AND INFORMATION

Many banks today offer computer services to prepare payrolls, monitor accounts receivable, and prepare checks for suppliers. Banks offer these services primarily to smaller companies and to branch offices that do not have their own computers.

Some banks offer time-shared computer services. With this service, a cash manager has a computer terminal in his or her office with direct access to the bank's computer. The cash manager can then immediately obtain such information as exact account balances, float reports, foreign exchange rates, and money market quotes. In addition, most bank time-sharing services offer programs to calculate cash flow, return on investment, and yields to maturity on bonds. Some banks also offer computer models for determining the best cities for a lockbox network.

COMPUTER SERVICES

Many banks now offer lockbox services to customers. With such a service, the company continues to bill customers, but customers send payments to a post office box. The bank opens the post office box as often as every hour and deposits all the received checks. Because lockboxes are usually located near customers, this system speeds up cash flow by reducing both mail float and check collection float.

Banks also provide regional concentration accounts. A company may establish several of these accounts around the country and then instruct each of its local branch offices to send each day's receipts to the nearest regional concentration account, usually by depository transfer check or by wire. At the end of each day, the regional concentration bank transfers by wire all funds above a certain minimum to the company's main headquarters account. Thus funds move quickly from a customer to a local branch office bank to a regional concentration bank to the company's main bank.

LOCKBOXES AND CONCENTRATION ACCOUNTS

Banks also help companies with foreign transactions. These services include:

FOREIGN TRANSACTIONS

1. Introducing companies to foreign business representatives.
2. Providing services at foreign branch or affiliate offices.
3. Providing advice on foreign business practices.
4. Financing exports and imports.
5. Conducting credit checks on potential customers or business associates.
6. Providing information about foreign economic conditions.

➤ BANK COMPENSATION

Banks can use several compensation methods to charge a customer for the services they provide. A cash manager should study these different forms of compensation and work with the bank to figure out which method or combination of methods will work best for the company.

Banks charge for their services in two basic ways: fees and minimum balances. Using the fee method, a bank sets a specific price on each of its services. Using the minimum balance method, a bank provides many services free but requires that the company maintain a specified minimum balance. For example, one bank may charge $0.10 for each check the company writes, $0.15 for each deposit, $0.03 for each deposit item, and so on. Another bank may charge nothing for these services but require that the company keep at least $200,000 in its checking account at all times.

DIRECT FEE VERSUS MINIMUM BALANCE

In general, cash managers prefer the fee approach because such fees are tax deductible. Every month, the bank itemizes the services it has provided and shows the price of each service. The company pays this bill and deducts the expense from its taxable income. Minimum balance requirements cost the company money because the company loses the income it could earn elsewhere on the balance. This lost income, however, is not deductible.

Banks generally prefer a minimum balance form of compensation for two reasons: (1) balances provide money for the bank to lend, and (2) growth in a bank is commonly measured by growth in deposits rather than sales (interest on loans, service fees, and so forth). The use of service fees has increased significantly in recent years. In the past, banks often underpriced their services and offered a correspondingly low earnings allowance on deposits. However, service fees have gradually increased so that they now reflect the bank's real costs. Likewise, the earnings allowance banks offer on demand accounts has risen in order to be competitive with alternative money market instruments.

At this time many banks offer companies a payment option on deposit account activity; that is, companies can pay either by maintaining balances or by paying fees of checks written, deposits made, and special services (such as stop-payment orders) requested. At the same time, many of these banks accept only fees (not balances) for specific services, such as handling trust accounts, data processing, and investment services. Because cash management services are deposit related, many banks offer companies the option of paying by fee or by maintaining a specified balance.

Since the Federal Reserve and the state bank authorities place differential reserve requirements on different types of accounts, the selection of the type of balance for the compensating balance becomes important. There are numerous possibilities, but the three major types are demand deposits, certificates of deposit, and repurchase agreements. If we assume that the Federal Reserve requires reserves of 12 percent to be held against demand deposits, 3 percent to be held against certificates of deposit, and 0 percent to be held against repurchase agreements, we can calculate the amount of money a firm has to put up to give the bank the same amount of usable funds, net of required reserves.

At this point, let us digress slightly to define repurchase agreements (repos). A repo is an agreement between a bank and a customer in which the customer agrees to buy a government security from the bank, and the bank agrees to buy back the same security at a predetermined price at a future date. In effect, the customer is providing funds to the bank, and the bank is giving the customer collateral until it repays the money to the customer. For this type of transaction, there are no required reserves if the total amount of repos the bank currently holds is less than or equal to the amount of repos they held on October 5, 1979. Otherwise, the reserve requirement is 10 percent.

Exhibit 6–1 shows the amount of funds required from the company for the bank to have the use of $300,000 as a compensating balance. It is apparent from this example that the amount of funds that the bank receives and the amount of funds the customer provides depend on the reserve requirement. By using repos instead of a certificate of deposit on a demand deposit account, the customer has use of an additional $9,000 or $36,000, respectively, while the funds available to the bank are $300,000 in all three instances. Clearly, using repos is one way of reducing the cost of borrowing for the customer and must be considered when determining whether fees or compensating balances are cheaper.

COMPENSATING BALANCES AND RESERVE REQUIREMENTS

	Repo	Certificate of Deposit	Demand Deposit
Funds available to bank	$300,000	$300,000	$300,000
Reserves required	0 (0%)	9,000 (3%)	36,000 (12%)
Customer funds provided	$300,000	$309,000	$336,000

Exhibit 6–1   Funds Required for Compensating Balances

Demand deposits are usually referred to as interest-free accounts to corporations. However, many banks offer an earnings allowance on at least part of a company's demand deposits, and this earnings allowance is, in effect, interest. The monthly earnings allowance pays for specific deposit-related activities, such as checks and deposits. If the earnings allowance exceeds these charges, the excess allowance is lost. If the earnings allowance is less than the monthly account charges, the customer pays the remaining charges in cash.

EARNINGS ALLOWANCE

Earnings allowances are usually very low compared to the rate the company could earn by investing excess funds in other investments. For example, a bank might offer a $0.15 earnings allowance per $100 of average monthly deposit. This $0.15 per month equals $1.80 per year on $100, or 1.8 percent.

Banks credit this earnings allowance on average collected funds. They do not credit for checks that have been deposited but have not yet cleared. Banks may not credit an earnings allowance for required compensating balances because these balances are theoretically designed to compensate the bank for making a loan, extending a line of credit, or providing another service.

Some banks subtract their own reserve requirements from a company's balance before calculating an earnings allowance. Reserve requirements are the funds that a bank must maintain in the Federal Reserve system, and they typically range from 9.0 to 14.5 percent of deposits.

In calculating an earnings allowance or in determining when a company's deposits will be available for the company's use, a bank estimates float. In this context, float is the time between when a check is deposited and when it is actually collected from the issuer's account. For smaller customers, banks often offer immediate availability of deposits. For larger customers, they calculate either an average float or an actual-days float.

FLOAT

Banks calculate an average float by determining the average number of days checks take to clear. For example, 50 percent of the checks a particular bank handles may clear in a day, 30 percent in two days, and so on. The bank then applies this average float time to all commercial accounts. For example, if a bank calculates its average float to be 1.5 days and a customer deposits a $10,000 check, $5,000 will be available one day after deposit, and the remaining $5,000 will be available on the second day. (Half in one day and half in two days equals 1.5 days average float.)

Although the average-days method is simpler for banks, it is not fair to all customers. For instance, a company depositing mostly cash and local checks (a supermarket, for example) does not have the full use of its cash as quickly as it should. On the other hand, a company depositing mostly out-of-town checks that require three or four days to collect, gains with the average-days method.

To solve this problem, some banks compute actual-days float by deferring the availability of deposited funds on an item-by-item basis. To do this, the bank examines each deposited check individually and determines the exact number of days it will take for the check to clear. The bank does this using a predetermined collection table, generally based on the Federal Reserve availability schedule.

Because of the work involved, few banks compute actual-days float by hand. Instead, they use a fully automated demand deposit accounting system, in which the collection time in days for each bank in the country is computer programmed. Float calculation is then automatic.

Time Deposits

Banks sometimes require compensation in the form of time deposits. Time deposits are noninterest-bearing certificates of deposit. Using this approach, the bank requires a customer to deposit, say, $100,000 for 90 days without interest. The bank then calculates the interest this money would earn at prevailing money market rates and credits this amount against the company's account activity charges. Banks prefer time deposits to balance requirements because the Federal Reserve sets lower reserve requirements on time deposits. A bank can lend $88,000 of a $100,000 *demand account balance* (the other $12,000 or 12 percent must remain in reserve), but it can lend $97,000 of a $100,000 *time deposit* (because only $3,000 or 3 percent must remain in reserve). Cash managers generally prefer demand deposit requirements because they can draw down their balance below the minimum requirement during part of the month and then deposit extra cash later to meet the average monthly balance requirement.

Tax Deposits

Every company must make monthly or quarterly tax deposits for social security and income tax payments. The corporation can pay these taxes directly to the U.S. Treasury Department or to any authorized bank. When a corporation pays an authorized bank, the funds usually remain in the bank a few days before they are withdrawn ("called") by the Treasury. Therefore, banks that receive these tax deposits benefit from free use of the money.

Cash managers have recognized the value of their tax payments and now request earnings credit on these deposits. Banks argue against giving an earnings credit on tax deposits for two reasons. First, the law requires companies to pay their taxes by specified dates. The money then no longer belongs to the company, and the company has no right to its earnings. Second, when the Treasury leaves money for a few extra days in a bank's tax accounts, the Treasury is actually compensating the bank for performing services such as tax collection bookkeeping. Again, the company has no right to these earnings.

Even though these reasons for opposing earnings credit on tax deposits may be valid, it is still true that companies have control over where they make their payments. When some banks in an area offer earnings credit on tax deposits, other banks in that area must make a similar offer to avoid losing all of their tax deposits.

Because these deposits are an important part of negotiating bank compensation, the cash manager should understand just what they are worth to a bank. From the tax deposit (say, $50,000), first subtract the reserve requirement on the amount (say, 12 percent). In this example, the net deposit is $41,875. Next, you must establish an interest rate. One rule of thumb uses the Treasury bill rate minus 1 percent. (The 1 percent compensates the bank for the securities it must leave on deposit with the Treasury Department in order to qualify as a special tax depository.) Finally, you must determine the average number of days the Treasury leaves tax deposits with the bank. If we assume a Treasury bill rate of 5 percent and an average of 10 days before the Treasury calls for tax deposits, the tax deposit is worth about $57 to the bank ($41,875 × 5% × 10 ÷ 365). If this deposit is made every month, the value in a year is 12 times as large, or $684. You may be able to convince a bank to apply at least part of these earnings toward your company's service charges.

Quite often, banks do not specify the exact minimum balance they expect from a customer; they just ask that it be reasonable. In such cases, some cash managers determine the balance they will maintain in the following way. They first establish a general level through discussion with bank officers. Then, over a period of months, they gradually reduce the average balance until someone at the bank complains. This approach does not strengthen the company-bank relationship, but as long as banks allow it, it usually results in the lowest possible balance requirements.

NEGOTIATING FEES AND REQUIRED BALANCES

Other cash managers use a more scientific technique. They carry out their own account analysis and estimate how profitable their account is to the bank. An account analysis shows the costs of all services rendered by the bank, the compensation received by the bank, and the net profit or loss to the bank. Exhibit 6–2 shows a typical account analysis that a bank uses. You can use the same form to see if you are a profitable customer of the bank. You must first estimate the amount the bank earned on the account during the month. Begin with the bank's average daily balance shown on its ledger and subtract the float (checks deposited but not yet cleared) using a two-day average float time and then subtract the reserve requirements (12 percent). This leaves the investable funds, which you can then multiply by the bank's annual earning rate, which you can estimate as the prime rate. Divide the earnings by 12 to get the bank's total earnings for the month from the account.

Next, you must estimate the cost to the bank of the services it provided during the month. Estimate the cost of each check and deposit by examining how much the bank charges individuals with checking accounts.

ACCOUNT ANALYSIS

I. **Demand deposit daily average:** Ledger $87,840.00   Collected $87,840.00

                          Less: Fed. Res. Bd. reserves @ 12%   10,540.80

    Average daily funds available: 77,299.20

                Credit @ 8.0% per annum   515.33

II. **Banking Services Performed**

	Unit Price	Volume	Amount
A. Standard services:			
Deposits processed	$ 0.56	36	$ 20.16
Items deposited	0.05	3000	150.00
Checks paid	0.15	3	0.45
Drafts paid			
Wire transfers	5.00	10	50.00
Collection items			
Coupon envelopes entered for collection			
Bonds entered for collection			
Security drafts entered for collection			
Returned items			
Stop payments	12.00	1	12.00
Treasurer's checks			
Certified checks	1.50	2	3.00
Coin rolling			
Payroll preparation			
Statements rendered	4.00	1	4.00
Other			
Subtotal			
B. Individualized services:			
Lockbox			
Data transmission			
Account reconcilement			
Safekeeping			
Computer			
Commercial paper — agent			
Other			
Subtotal			
C. Investment and/or advisory services:			
Credit information			
Investment advice			
International			
Proxy			
Computer			
Other			
Subtotal			
Total services that have been priced			$ 239.61
Account position as a result			$ 275.72

Exhibit 6–2   Account Analysis for ABC Corporation, August 1991

Find out the number of checks written and the number of deposits made by looking at the company's monthly account statement. Estimate the cost of special services (such as credit reference checks or newsletters) at approximately the price charged by similar outside services.

Finally, income minus cost of services gives the profit (or loss) to the bank. If the account appears too profitable to the bank, you can safely reduce your company's average balance.

Cash managers find that many banks are willing to prepare this account analysis for company review. By understanding the source of each item in the account analysis, the cash manager can successfully negotiate a realistic minimum average cash balance for the company.

PROFITABILITY ANALYSIS

Profitability analysis seeks to overcome some of the shortcomings of regular account analysis by presenting considerably more detailed income statements for major customers. Multiple accounts for a single corporate relationship are consolidated, including those of subsidiaries and perhaps even major officers. Losses on one account, therefore, can be offset with profits on others. The earnings and expenses associated with loans and various fee services, such as the purchase and sale of securities not typically considered in an account analysis are likely to be included in a profitability statement. Rather than emphasizing activity charges, however, profitability analysis focuses on the commercial lending function of banks and is of the greatest use in determining the profitability of net borrowers.

In the profitability analysis, the net amount of funds borrowed is computed, and the estimated profit or loss from the income statement is generally assumed to raise or lower the return on funds loaned. Since estimated profitability tends to be strongly influenced by the terms on loans—compensating balances, interest rates, and associated fees—the analysis has often been proposed as a means of determining the loan terms necessary to meet a minimum profit goal for a bank. It can also be a helpful guide in allocating bank resources, since the analysis tends to highlight the most profitable types of customers and loans. In some banks, the analysis is also used to evaluate the performance of lending officers.

The first section of the profitability statement in Exhibit 6–3 contains an analysis of the sources and uses of bank funds. Multiple loans to a customer are first consolidated to obtain average loan balances (line 1).

As in the account analysis, average investable or loanable funds provided to the bank by the customer (line 4) are obtained by deducting cash items in process of collection and an allowance for reserve requirements from gross ledger balances. Some banks also make deductions for the compensating balances required to cover the activity charges in the account analysis. Regardless, the deposit figure remaining after the various deductions have been subtracted is then netted against average loans outstanding to obtain the average net bank funds used by the customer (line 5). The customer, in other words, is assumed to borrow his own funds first.

For many banks, the previous step completes the analysis of bank funds advanced to a customer. If the bank, however, wishes to relate the profit on the relationship to the return on bank capital, as is the case in the

ACCOUNT: XYZ COMPANY
AFFILIATED ACCOUNTS: AB
                       CD
                       EF

DATE: 20 OCT. 19XX
PERIOD: 1 JAN.–30 SEPT.

	CURRENT PERIOD	LAST 12 MONTHS
SOURCES AND USES OF FUNDS		
1. Average loan balance:	$____	$____
2. Average collected balance:	$____	$____
a. Investable balance (17.5% reserve):	$____	$____
3. Average time balance:	$____	$____
a. Investable balance (3% reserve):	$____	$____
4. Total loanable funds (2a + 3a):	$____	$____
5. Bank funds used by customer (1 − 4):	$____	$____
a. Allocated capital (8% of 1):	$____	$____
b. Funds transferred from pool (5 − 5a):	$____	$____
INCOME		
6. Gross interest income on loans:	$____	$____
7. Earnings on deposits (xxx% of 4):	$____	$____
8. Fees paid:		
a: Service charge fees:	$____	$____
b: Loan commitments:	$____	$____
c: Data processing:	$____	$____
d: Total (8a + 8b + 8c):	$____	$____
9. Total income (6 + 7 + 8):	$____	$____
EXPENSES		
10. Activity costs from account analysis:	$____	$____
11. Interest accrued on time deposits:	$____	$____
12. Charge for bank funds used:		
a: Allocated capital (20% of 5a):	$____	$____
b: Pool funds (xxx% of 5b):	$____	$____
c: Total (12a + 12b):	$____	$____
13. Loan handling expenses:	$____	$____
14. Cost of fee services:	$____	$____
15. Data processing:	$____	$____
16. Total expenses (10 + 11 + 12 + 13 + 14 + 15):	$____	$____
NET INCOME		
17. Net income before taxes (9 − 16):	$____	$____
PROFITABILITY MEASURES		
18. Allocated capital index (17 ÷ 5a):	____%	____%
19. Net profits/net funds used (17 ÷ 5):	____%	____%
20. Net profits/gross amount borrowed (17 ÷ 1):	____%	____%
21. Gross profits/net funds used [(17 + 12c) ÷ 5]:	____%	____%

EXHIBIT 6–3   PROFITABILITY ANALYSIS

example, the net funds loaned to the customer must be subdivided into at least two categories. The first is the proportion of funds supplied from the bank's capital account. Allocated capital (line 5a) is frequently a flat percentage of gross loans. Some banks, though, assign capital in proportion to the estimated risk on loans, while others assume capital is also required to support the customer's deposits. Since profits will ultimately be related to the assigned capital, variations in its allocation can have a significant impact on the estimated profitability of a relationship. All other things being equal, a higher capital allocation tends to reduce the profit rate. In any event, if the return on capital is to be a measure of actual profitability, the capital assigned to a customer relationship should be selected in such a way that for the bank as a whole the total assigned capital is equal to the bank's actual capital.

The remaining category of bank funds supplied (line 5b) is a residual and represents funds obtained from sources other than the capital accounts. If the bank chooses to differentiate further among alternative sources of funds, such as purchased funds and deposit funds, this entry could be subdivided. The use of multiple pools of funds, however, is relatively uncommon.

The second section of the profitability statement lists the major sources of income derived by the bank from the customer relationship. Most of the entries shown are self-explanatory.

The third major section deals with the bank's total expenses associated with servicing the customer relationship.

The last lines of the profitability statement are used to derive different indicators of the profitability of the customer relationship. Total profits or net income is shown on line 17. On line 18, the allocated capital index is computed by dividing profit by allocated capital. If greater than zero, this index indicates that the bank is actually realizing a higher profit rate on customer relationships than the goal previously established by the bank. A negative figure would suggest that profits were not sufficient to meet that target, while a zero figure would imply the goal had just been met.

➤ CRITERIA USED IN SELECTING BANKS

A large national company requires three types of banks to handle all its needs. For example, local banks are needed for handling the receipts, and possibly the disbursements, of local branch offices. A large company with nationwide branches also has to select regional concentration banks for collecting funds from all the local branch office banks in its area and, sometimes, for channeling disbursement funds to branch offices. Finally, such a company needs the services of one or more main corporate banks, usually in the corporate headquarters city.

A company uses the same six criteria to select any of the types of banks just described. However, the importance of these criteria varies considerably depending on which type of bank is being evaluated. The six most important criteria are:

1. Location.
2. Size, including the bank's resources, operating record, and financial standing.
3. Type of bank, either wholesale, retail, or a combination.
4. Services offered, including staff expertise.
5. Costs of services.
6. Management, including management quality and philosophy, industry knowledge, concern for the company, and personal rapport.

How important is a bank's location? For disbursing cash, the more remote the bank, the better because its checks clear slowly and provide both the company and the bank with extra cash. However, the right location is essential for efficient cash gathering.

BANK LOCATION

PROXIMITY TO MAIN POST OFFICE

If the bank receives deposits by mail (through either a lockbox system or the receipt of depository transfer checks from branch offices), it must be close to the main post office in its district. This allows frequent messenger trips to the post office throughout the day (often hourly) so that incoming mail can be processed. If a bank must wait for its mail to be delivered to a branch post office, it will lose many hours of processing time every day.

PROXIMITY TO FEDERAL RESERVE BANK

To understand the importance of location to check collection, it is useful to understand how banks collect checks using the Federal Reserve system. The Federal Reserve system consists of 12 districts throughout the country, 12 reserve banks (one in the principal city of each district), and 24 branch banks (from zero to four branches in each district). These 36 banks form a national network so that any bank in the country can collect the checks it receives.

In practice, each bank sorts the checks it receives and physically moves the checks to the nearest Federal Reserve bank. The Federal Reserve banks (including branches) transfer checks among themselves by plane and then distribute the checks to the original issuing banks in their area.

Funds from checks deposited with a Federal Reserve bank or branch are available either the same day, in one day, or in two days. The exact time depends on both the location of the original issuing bank and the time of day the check was deposited with the Federal Reserve system. For example, checks written on a Providence bank and deposited before 3:00 P.M. with the Boston Federal Reserve Bank are available the same day. If the same check is deposited after 3:00 P.M., the funds become available the following day. The Federal Reserve has set these deadlines throughout the day and early evening after evaluating the time required to prove (verify), sort, and physically move checks to the districts and banks on which they were drawn in time to meet local deadlines.

You can see now why a bank's location can be so important. If a bank misses a Federal Reserve deadline, all funds are tied up an extra day, but proximity to a Federal Reserve bank allows extra processing time. For example, a bank in downtown Atlanta can process checks up to half an hour before each Federal Reserve deadline and still make delivery to the Federal Reserve bank on time. A suburban Atlanta bank might have to stop processing deposited checks two hours before the deadline, and a Macon bank (100 miles from Atlanta) might require a cutoff time four hours before the deadline.

PROXIMITY TO MAJOR AIRPORT

Although the Federal Reserve network clears most of the checks in the banking system, many banks clear some checks directly between themselves. For instance, if a Boston bank regularly clears a large dollar volume of checks through a specific New York bank, these two banks may make arrangements to clear checks directly between themselves and thereby gain an entire night of extra processing time. In this case, the Boston Federal Reserve deadline for next day availability of funds for New York City checks is 10:30 P.M. By making direct arrangements with the New York City bank, the Boston bank can put its checks on the first Boston-to-New York flight the following morning at 7:00 A.M. and still achieve the same availability. Because the airlines carry checks between banks with direct clearing arrangements, access to a major airport is essential for any bank trying to speed up its check collection ability.

EFFICIENT CHECK COLLECTION

In conclusion, therefore, companies will find the most efficient check-collecting banks near a major post office, near a Federal Reserve bank or branch, and near a major airport. Nearly all the banks meeting these criteria are located in the 36 Federal Reserve cities listed in Exhibit 6–4. A company's *regional concentration banks* and its *main bank* will almost always be located in these cities. Local banks must be near the company's local branch offices and near its local customers for fast check collection.

SIZE OF BANK

The size of a bank's assets is one measure of its ability to provide services. A small bank, even one with an ideal location, simply cannot collect checks as quickly as a large, well-organized bank. A small bank cannot provide 24 hourly pickups a day at the post office, nor can it justify a three-shift check collection operation.

What determines adequate size? One rule of thumb requires that a bank's assets exceed $500 million. Only 3 percent of the country's banks are this size, yet they process over 60 percent of all deposited checks. Because of the high volume of checks per bank, most of these banks are organized to collect checks quickly and efficiently.

The remaining 40 percent of deposited checks are cleared by 97 percent of the country's banks. Here, the number of checks per bank is relatively small, and these banks generally cannot clear checks as quickly. These smaller banks either deposit checks with correspondent banks for collec-

District	Reserve Banks	Branches
1	Boston	
2	New York	Buffalo
3	Philadelphia	
4	Cleveland	Cincinnati Pittsburgh
5	Richmond	Baltimore Charlotte, N.C.
6	Atlanta	Birmingham Jacksonville Nashville New Orleans
7	Chicago	Detroit
8	St. Louis	Little Rock Louisville Memphis
9	Minneapolis	Helena
10	Kansas City	Denver Oklahoma City Omaha
11	Dallas	El Paso Houston San Antonio
12	San Francisco	Los Angeles Portland Salt Lake City Seattle

Exhibit 6–4   Federal Reserve Banks and Branches

tion or rely heavily on the Federal Reserve banks' facilities. Both these methods slow down the availability of collected funds.

The rule of thumb of $500 million in assets is only a guideline, or screen. You should judge each bank's capabilities individually. Local banks need not pass such a stringent test. A local bank of much smaller size, but with a solid operating record and healthy finances, is fully satisfactory.

One method of classifying banks is by the type of customers they seek. *Retail* or personal banks seek individual consumers as customers, whereas the customers of *wholesale* banks are business firms. The third classification by customer is the *combination* bank that serves the needs of both individuals and businesses. Personal (retail) banks usually have small assets and primarily service personal checking and savings accounts. Business (wholesale) banks have larger assets and primarily service industrial, commercial,

Type of Bank

agricultural, and export–import accounts. Combination banks include almost all the largest banks in the country, and they solicit both business and personal accounts. Combination banks usually have a large office in the downtown business district and branch offices in outlying districts and suburbs. These branches often specialize in personal accounts, whereas most of the bank's business experts work in the main downtown office.

Companies must recognize the difference between personal and business activities to establish a satisfactory banking relationship. Very often, smaller companies mistakenly open accounts with consumer banks or with the consumer-oriented branches of combination banks. They consequently find lending officers who are more oriented toward home mortgages and car loans than to business loans, and the banking relationship suffers. Larger companies always have the correct type of bank for their main corporate account, but their local branch offices around the country sometimes choose the wrong type of bank because they do not realize that there are different types of banks.

SERVICES

Banks today offer a wide variety of services. In selecting a bank, a company must be certain that the bank offers all the services the company requires (lockbox, wire transfer, and so forth) as well as a reasonable range of the services that the company may require in the future. The cash manager should also verify the bank staff's expertise in providing services by reviewing staff credentials and checking with customers who use the bank's other services.

COSTS

Bank costs vary widely. Banks in the same market often charge different rates for similar services, and they may prefer payment in different ways (fees or balances). To obtain the greatest value, a company must carefully compare the services offered by each bank in the market and the costs for these services.

MANAGEMENT

In selecting a main corporate bank or an important regional concentration bank, a company should also evaluate the bank's management. Bank management includes both the specific company contact officer and the bank's overall management. Management factors, which include management philosophy, management quality, industrial knowledge, concern for the company, and the personal relationships between the bank and the company personnel involved, are considerably more subjective than the other selection criteria.

➤ COMMUNICATING WITH BANK CONTACT OFFICERS

To establish rapport with any banker, a financial manager must understand the banker's needs. A banker's most important need is to understand the financial condition of his or her customers. Therefore, you should make sure that your bank contact officer receives regular financial statements from your company, including both income statements and balance sheets. Smaller companies usually send these reports quarterly, whereas larger companies send them monthly.

There are two advantages to sending regular financial statements, even when there is no loan outstanding. First, it saves the banker the necessity of asking for them. Second, it assures the banker that he or she will continue receiving regular financial statements after a loan is granted.

In addition to receiving income statements and balance sheets (which show company history), bankers like to receive company forecasts. The most useful are earnings forecasts, projected balance sheets, and cash forecasts. A cash forecast is particularly important if it shows the need for a bank loan later in the year. Such a forecast will show clearly how the need for a loan develops, when the loan will be needed, and how large a loan will be required. This information makes it possible to negotiate the loan in advance rather than at the last minute.

In addition to receiving financial information, bankers need to confer fairly regularly with important officers in the company. This enables the banker to ask specific questions about operations and to judge the continuing quality and commitment of the management team. Typically, the treasurer or some other high-level member of the financial staff meets with the bank contact officer monthly or quarterly (when delivering financial statements). The president and other senior executives typically meet with the banker once or twice a year.

> ## Evaluating Bank Performance

Just as banks evaluate companies, companies must regularly evaluate their banks. Banks should be formally judged by company treasurers at least once a year on three criteria: the banks' performance of contracted services, the quality of their advice and new ideas, their costs relative to other banks, and the degree of soundness of the bank.

Performance of contracted services can be evaluated objectively and should include the following three areas:

1. *Speed.* (Were lockboxes, wire transfers, deposits, and reports all functioning at the agreed-on pace?)
2. *Reliability.* (Was the bank consistently fast?)
3. *Accuracy.* (Did the bank commit a minimum number of errors?)

Advice and attitude are subjective but may be judged with respect to the following two factors:

1. *Quality of consulting and investment advice, if required.* (A banker should offer fast, accurate, and thoughtful advice on banking matters. A bank may or may not offer investment advice, depending on its agreements with the company.)

2. *Rapport.* (A banker should have a strong interest in the company and its managers as well as reasonable knowledge about its business.)

After rating the bank on these objective and subjective factors, a company should compare the bank's performance with its costs. The company should also compare the prices of its bank with the prices of competing banks to make sure that the company is obtaining the best value.

Perhaps one of the more important considerations we face during the decade of the 1990s is the financial soundness of the banking institutions with which we do business. It must be remembered that banks as financial intermediaries cannot immediately pay off all of their debt and deposits. Two of the principal functions of a financial intermediary are to provide maturity transformation and to provide liquidity transformation. In short, the purpose of a bank is to borrow short (deposits) and lend long (loans), and to hold assets (loans and investments), which are less liquid than the bank's liabilities (deposits). Hence, at any time loans and investments that are maturing will be insufficient to meet all of the bank's liquidity requirements. However, over a given period of time, if the bank is to remain solvent, all liabilities must be paid off. It is the job of the bank regulators to ensure that the depositors are protected from the problem of bank insolvency up to a certain point ($100,000). However, the inconvenience of not receiving the services of the bank can adversely affect the company's cash management. Therefore, the company should evaluate the potential solvency or insolvency of the bank with which it does business on a periodic basis.

Ratios and financial analyses have been developed to analyze banks in the areas of profitability, capital, liquidity, and asset risk. Like all such analyses, the ratios of the bank in question should be evaluated in terms of a peer group of similar banks and also evaluated over time for any signs of deterioration of the bank's creditworthiness.

Profitability measures generally are an important indicator of bank management competence, which is very important to the long-run solvency of the bank. Ratios such as return on assets (ROA) and return on risk assets (RORA) are two of the more important measures. ROA is defined as net operating earnings divided by average amount of total assets. RORA is defined as net operating earnings divided by loans, leases, non-U.S. government securities, and other risky assets.

The capital adequacy of a bank is for the market and the regulators one of the most important factors in a bank's ability to maintain customer confidence. An inadequately capitalized bank faces regulatory and market pressure to restrain growth of assets and services. Capital adequacy is measured by such ratios as equity divided by loans or by equity divided by risk assets. Also, equity as a percentage of total assets is important. The main function of equity capital in a bank is to act as a common cushion to absorb losses or shrinkages in value of the various assets of the bank. Loans are probably the bank's riskiest asset, therefore the equity to loan ratio is given special attention.

Liquidity serves a dual function for banks. First the bank must be liquid to meet any expected or unexpected shrinkage in deposits. Second, the bank must be liquid if it is to meet an expanding demand for loans and/or services, increase its investments, and take advantage of fluctuations in the interest rate cycle. Ironically, cash, or at least a great portion of it, may not be available to meet the liquidity needs of a bank. A bank's cash is composed of vault cash, required reserves, and float. A certain amount of vault cash is necessary to meet the daily needs of the bank; the required reserves cannot be used to meet liquidity needs, and it is very difficult for the bank to alter the pattern of float. Therefore, cash is not a good measure of a bank's liquidity.

U.S. government securities, if they are unpledged, are generally a bank's principal liquid asset. A key characteristic of T-bills is their marketability. Hence, a good measure of liquidity for a bank would be the percentage of unpledged T-bills to total assets or total investments. Other money market investments such as time deposits in other banks, CDs, federal funds, and commercial paper can provide a degree of liquidity and should be evaluated on a case-by-case basis.

The riskiness of the assets held by the bank are of major importance in evaluating the quality of the entire bank. Recent experiences with loan losses and write-offs may be an indication of a risky situation. Banks with a low ratio of loan loss divided by total loans tend to retain this low-risk profile over time, while banks with a high loan loss ratio tend to maintain this risky position over time. Therefore, past experience may be a good indicator of future performance.

There are various outside sources that provide quality ratings for commercial banks usually based on an adaptation of the above type of analysis. Such firms as Standard & Poor's and Moody's rate the long-term debt issued by the individual banks. Keefe, Buyette, and Woods and Sheshunoff rate the quality of the banks themselves.

➤ Summary

In this chapter, we examined many aspects of bank services, charges, and relations. Banks today still provide traditional services, such as checking accounts, savings accounts, and loans. However, they also offer new services, such as financial advice, computer services, lockboxes, concentration accounts, and assistance with foreign transactions. Banks charge for their services, either through fees (a charge for each piece of work performed) or by requiring a company to maintain a specified interest-free checking account balance.

We discussed ways of negotiating service charges with banks, including using tax deposits as a bargaining tool. Finally, we examined the six criteria used in selecting banks: location, size, type of bank, services, costs, and management. We also presented a financial analysis framework for evaluating the soundness of a commercial bank.

CHAPTER 7

SOURCES OF SHORT-TERM CASH

By the end of this chapter, the reader will be able to:

LEARNING OBJECTIVES

1. Analyze credit terms and the cost of trade credit.
2. Describe how a company can alter its sales terms to collect cash more quickly.
3. Discuss the key features of short-term bank loans.
4. Describe the use of commercial paper as an alternative to short-term bank loans.
5. Differentiate between pledging and factoring receivables.
6. Discuss the various types of loans against the firm's inventory.

Companies do not have all the cash they need all the time. Very often, a company needs to build up its inventory; this can reduce its cash levels. Or a company's customers may place unusually large orders, and the need to finance the additional accounts receivable will reduce a company's cash level. In this chapter, therefore, we describe the many ways companies obtain additional short-term cash to restore their cash balances to the required levels. As a rule, financial managers look for short-term cash at the lowest possible rates. If they cannot obtain cash at no cost or at a very small cost, they begin to explore more expensive sources of cash. For example, a financial manager faced with a cash shortage might look first to the company's suppliers and its customers. He or she would look to suppliers because they extend credit to the company by collecting for goods and services *after* those goods and services are supplied. The cash manager can enlarge this credit by paying bills more slowly. The cash manager may also obtain additional cash by collecting from the company's customers more quickly.

If these relatively low-cost options are unavailable (or if their cost is too high because of the ill will generated), the cash manager may next turn to the company's bank for a short-term loan. In this chapter, we examine loan applications, terms of typical loans, and bank relations. In addition, larger companies have access to the commercial paper market, which we also discuss.

Companies faced with a severe cash shortage may also try to convert into cash two of their working capital assets—accounts receivable and inventory. A company may pledge its accounts receivable to a finance company in exchange for a loan, or it may sell its accounts receivable to a factoring company for cash. Similarly, a company may pledge its inventory (often using a warehousing system) in exchange for a loan.

➤ Trade Credit

Trade credit is one important and often low-cost source of cash. Nearly all companies make use of trade credit to some degree by not paying suppliers immediately for goods and services. Instead, suppliers bill the company, and the company pays in 10 days, 30 days, or more. From the time when the supplier first provides the goods or services to the time when the customer finally pays for them, the supplier has, in effect, loaned the company money. The sum of all these loans (bills) represents a company's trade credit. By paying bills more slowly, a company can increase the amount of these loans from its suppliers.

One way a company can take more time to pay its bills (or stretch its payables) is to stop taking discounts. For example, if your company normally takes advantage of all prompt-payment discounts, such as 2 percent for payment within 10 days, you can increase your company's cash by passing up the discount and paying the bill in the expected 30 days. Of course, this is an expensive source of cash. If you lose a 2 percent discount and have the use of the funds for 20 more days, you have paid approximately 36 percent interest (annual rate) for using the money.

Calculating True Costs

However, you might argue that, in practice, the interest cost would not really be 36 percent because a company forgoing its discounts and aggressively stretching its payables would not pay the bill in 30 days. Instead, such a company would stretch out this payable as long as possible and perhaps attempt to pay in 60 days. Now, the equivalent interest rate is only about 15 percent (50 days' extra use of the money for 2 percent).

This brings up the subject of late payments. Many cash managers do not consider 30 days (or any other stated terms) a real deadline. Instead, they try to determine the exact point at which further delay of payment will have a penalty. For example, if a company pays too slowly, the supplier may require payment in full on future orders; report the company to a credit bureau, which would damage the company's credit rating with all suppliers; or even bring legal action against the company. Many cash managers believe, however, that as long as they can pay company bills just before incurring any of these penalties, they maximize their company's cash at little or no cost. The hidden costs of this approach include such risks as damaged reputation, lower credit limit from suppliers, higher prices from suppliers to compensate for delayed payment, and the risk of exceeding the supplier's final deadline and incurring a penalty.

If you want more trade credit and want to stretch out your payables, you do not always have to incur the risks just described. Very often, you can negotiate with your suppliers for more generous credit terms, at least temporarily. If you and your supplier agree on longer credit terms (say 60 days or even 90 days), you get the extra trade credit you need without jeopardizing your supplier relations or credit ratings.

Negotiating With Suppliers

Keep in mind that suppliers are trying to build up their businesses and must compete with other similar suppliers. One way these suppliers compete is through credit terms, and this can be used to advantage. Just as you get several price quotes before placing a major order, you may also want to encourage competition among suppliers for credit terms.

Some suppliers use generous terms of trade credit as a form of sales promotion. This is especially likely where a distributor is trying to enter a new geographical area and is faced with the need to lure customers away from established rivals. In such circumstances, generous credit may well be more effective than an intensive advertising campaign or a high-pressure sales team. The credit may be a simple extension of the discount and/or net terms, or it may take a modified form such as an inventory loan.

If you are in a highly seasonal business, such as many types of retailing, you will find large differences in credit terms in different seasons. For example, as a retailer, you might be very short of cash in the fall as you build up for the Christmas selling season. Many suppliers will understand this and willingly will extend their normal 30-day terms.

Seasonal Business

Furthermore, some suppliers will offer exceedingly generous credit terms in order to smooth out their own manufacturing cycle. Consider a game manufacturer who sells half its annual production in the few months before Christmas. Rather than produce and ship most of the games in the late summer, this manufacturer would much rather spread out its production and shipping schedule over most of the year. To accomplish this, the manufacturer may offer seasonal dating to its retail store customers. Seasonal dating provides longer credit terms on orders placed in off-peak periods. For example, the game manufacturer might offer a 120-day terms on May orders, 90-day terms on June orders, and so on. This will encourage customers to order early, and it will allow the game manufacturer to spread out production over more of the year.

Trade credit has two important advantages that justify extensive use of it. The first advantage is convenience and ready availability; because it is not negotiated, it requires no great expenditure of executive time and no legal expenses. If a supplier accepts a company as a customer, the usual credit terms are automatically extended even though the maximum line of credit may be set low at first. The second advantage, which is closely related to the first, is that *the credit available from this source automatically grows as the company grows*. As sales expand, production schedules are increased. This in turn means that larger quantities of materials and supplies must be bought. In the absence of limits on credit, the additional credit becomes

Advantages of Trade Credit

available automatically simply by placing orders for the extra material. Of course, if the manufacturing process is long and the supplier's payment deadline is reached before the goods have been sold, some additional source of credit will also be needed. But the amount required will still be very much less than it would have been if no trade credit had been available.

➤ Tightening up Accounts Receivable Collections

Rapidly growing accounts receivable tie up a company's money and can cause a cash squeeze. However, these same accounts receivable become cash when they are collected. How can receivables be collected more quickly? From Chapter 5, you know the techniques (such as lockboxes and wire transfers) used to collect receivables quickly and regularly, so the real question is: How can the rate of collection of receivables be increased temporarily during a cash shortage?

The most effective way to collect receivables quickly is simply to ask for the money. If you just send a bill every month and show the amount past due, the customer may not feel a great pressure to pay quickly. But if you ask for the money, either with a handwritten note on the statement of account, a phone call, or a formal letter, the customer will usually pay more quickly. To take an extreme case, a customer receiving several calls a week from an aggressive cash manager may pay the bill just to get the cash manager to stop bothering him. Of course, these more aggressive collection techniques also have costs, such as loss of customer goodwill, scaring away new customers, loss of old customers to more lenient suppliers, and the generation of industry rumors that the company is short of cash and may be a poor credit risk.

You can see that stretching out accounts payable and collecting accounts receivable more quickly are really two sides of the same issue. Most companies try to stretch out their bill payments as long as is reasonably possible and to collect their own bills as quickly as competitively possible. Your objective as a cash manager is to maximize company cash, using both these techniques, without antagonizing either suppliers or customers so much that your working relationship with them suffers.

As we have just seen, the fastest way to collect receivables is to ask for the money regularly. However, a company can also change its sales terms to collect cash more quickly. Companies have several options including:

1. *Introduce discounts.* A company can initiate a discount for prompt payment (for example, a 2 percent discount for payment within ten days). Similarly, a company with an existing discount may increase the discount (for example, increase discount from 1 to 2 percent).
2. *Reduce credit terms.* If competitively possible, a company may require payment in full in 15 days, a deposit when the order is placed, COD orders (in which the customer must pay for goods on delivery), or even full payment with the order. Companies will have difficulty insti-

tuting these measures if competitors offer significantly more lenient credit terms.

3. *Emphasize cash sales*. Some companies, particularly those selling directly to consumers, may be able to increase their percentage of cash sales.

4. *Accept credit cards*. Sales made on bank credit cards (such as Master Card or Visa) or on travel or entertainment cards (such as American Express or Diners Club) are convertible within a couple of days into cash. The credit card companies charge 3 to 7 percent of the amount of the sale for this service.

5. *Impose a penalty for late payment*. Some companies now charge 1.0 or 1.5 percent of the unpaid balance per month as a penalty for late payment. Again, competitive conditions may make this approach impossible.

➤ SHORT-TERM BANK LOANS

After a company has fully used its trade credit and collected its receivables as quickly as competitively possible, it may turn to a bank for a short-term loan. The most common bank loan is a short-term, unsecured loan made for 90 days. Standard variations include loans made for periods of 30 days to a year and loans requiring collateral. Interest charges on these loans typically vary from the prime rate (the amount a bank charges its largest and most financially strong customers) to about 3 percent above prime.

Very often, a company doesn't immediately need money but can forecast that it will have a definite need in, say, six months. This company would not want to borrow the required money now and pay unnecessary interest for the next six months. Instead, the company would formally apply to its bank for a line of credit—that is, an assurance by the bank that, as long as the company remains financially healthy, the bank will lend the company money (up to a specified limit) whenever the company needs it. Banks usually review a company's credit line each year. A line of credit is not a guarantee that the bank will make a loan in the future. Instead, when the company actually needs the money, the bank will examine the company's current financial statements to make sure that actual results coincide with earlier plans.

LINE OF CREDIT

Banks also grant guaranteed lines of credit. Under this arrangement, the bank guarantees to supply funds up to a specified limit, regardless of circumstances. This relieves the company of any worries that money may not be available when it is needed. Banks usually charge extra for this guarantee, typically 1 percent a year on the unused amount of the guaranteed line of credit. For example, if the bank guarantees a credit line of $1 million and the company borrows only $300,000, the company will have to pay a commitment fee of perhaps $7,000 for the $700,000 it did not borrow.

In return for granting lines of credit, banks usually require that the company maintain a compensating balance (that is, keep a specified amount in its checking account without interest). For example, if a company receives a $1 million line of credit with the requirement that it maintain a 15 percent compensating balance, the company must keep at least $150,000 in its demand account with that bank all year. The bank, of course, does not have to pay interest on this demand account money; so the use of this money is the bank's compensation for standing ready to grant up to $1 million in loans for a year. Of course, when the bank actually makes loans during the year, it charges the negotiated rate of interest on the loan.

The line of credit usually has a set of conditions or covenants associated with it that spells out in detail the terms of the agreement. The covenants may be of a positive nature (e.g., the company must maintain a current ratio of one or a set amount of working capital), or they may be of a negative nature (e.g., setting a limit on the degree of management salary increases or payment of dividends to shareholders). The purpose of the covenants is to spell out the degree of control the bank may exercise given that they are lending money to the company.

Maturity of Loans

The most common time period, or maturity, for short-term bank loans is 90 days; however, a company can negotiate maturities of 30 days to one year. Banks often prefer 90-day maturities, even when the company will clearly need the money for longer than 90 days, because the three-month maturity gives the bank a chance to check the company's financial statements regularly. If the company's position has deteriorated, the bank can refuse to renew the loan and, therefore, avoid a future loss. Companies, on the other hand, prefer maturities that closely match the time they expect to need the money. A longer maturity, rather than a series of short, constantly renewed loans, eliminates the possibility that the bank will refuse to extend a short-term loan because of a temporary weakness in the company's operations.

Lines of credit are usually negotiated for a one-year period. However, a revolving line of credit can be set up for up to three years. During this period, the company may borrow funds as needed up to a certain amount and pay off their borrowings when they experience surplus cash flow. Since the revolving line of credit can be rolled over for additional two- or three-year periods, this facility for borrowing and repaying at the option of the company becomes almost a permanent source of short-term liquidity.

Interest Rates

The rates of interest charged by commercial banks vary in two ways: The general level of interest rates varies over time, and at any given time, different rates are charged to different borrowers. The base rate for most commercial banks traditionally has been the prime rate although with soaring market interest rates some of the larger banks are experimenting with marginal pricing schemes. The *prime rate* is the rate that commercial banks charge their very best business customers for short-term borrowing. It is the rate that the financial press puts on the front page every time it is changed. Congress and the business community speculate about the prime's influence on economic activity because it is the base line for loan pricing in most loan agreements.

Historically, the prime was a base line for loan pricing; "prime plus two" or "120 percent of prime" was a normal statement of interest rate on many loan contracts. However, as the banking industry has begun to price its loans and services more aggressively, the prime is becoming less important. Along with the change in the prime, compensating balances (the borrower's agreeing to hold a certain percentage of the amount of the loan in a noninterest-bearing account) are becoming less popular. The current trend in loan pricing is to price the loan at a rate above the marginal cost of funds as typically reflected by the interest rates on certificates of deposit. The bank then adds an interest rate margin to the cost of funds, and the sum becomes the rate charged to the borrower. This rate changes daily in line with the changes on money market rates offered by the bank. As liability management becomes more of a way of life for bankers, the pricing of loans will become a function of the amount of competition, both domestic and international, that the banker faces in securing loanable funds. As a result of this competition for corporate customers and enhanced competition from the commercial paper market, large, financially stable corporations are often able to borrow at a rate below prime.

Interest represents the price that borrowers pay to the bank for credit over specified periods of time. The amount of interest paid depends on a number of factors: the dollar amount of the loan, the length of time involved, the nominal annual rate of interest, the repayment schedule, and the method used to calculate the interest.

The various methods used to calculate interest are all variations of the simple interest calculation. *Simple interest* is calculated on the amount borrowed for the length of time the loan is outstanding. If $1 million is borrowed at 15 percent and repaid in one payment at the end of one year, the simple interest would be $1 million times 0.15, or $150,000.

When the *add-on interest method* is used, interest is calculated on the full amount of the original principal. The interest amount is immediately added to the original principal, and payments are determined by dividing principal plus interest by the number of payments to be made. When only one payment is involved, this method is identical to simple interest. However, when two or more payments are to be made, the use of this method results in an effective rate of interest that is greater than the nominal rate. In our example above, if the $1 million loan were repaid in two six-month installments of $575,000 each, the effective rate is higher than 15 percent because the borrower does not have the use of funds for the entire year.

The *bank discount method* is commonly used with short-term business loans. Generally, there are no immediate payments, and the life of the loan is usually one year or less. Interest is calculated on the amount of the loan, and the borrower receives the difference between the amount to be paid back and the amount of interest. In our example, the effective interest rate is 17.6 percent. The interest amount of $150,000 is subtracted from the $1 million, and the borrower has the use of $850,000 for one year. If we divide the interest payment by the amount of money actually used by the borrower ($150,000 divided by $850,000), we find the effective rate to be 17.6 percent.

If the loan were to require a compensating balance of 10 percent, the borrower does not have the use of the entire loan amount; rather, the borrower has the use of the loan amount less the compensating balance requirement. The effective rate of interest in this case would be 20 percent—the interest amount of $150,000 divided by the funds available, which is $750,000 ($1,000,000 minus $150,000 interest and minus a compensating balance of $100,000). The effective interest cost on a revolving credit agreement includes both interest costs and the commitment fee. Assume, for example, the TBA Corporation has a $1 million revolving credit agreement with a bank. Interest on the borrowed funds is 15 percent per annum. TBA must pay a commitment fee of 1 percent on the unused portion of the credit line. If the firm borrows $500,000, the effective annual interest rate is 16 percent [(0.15 × $500,000) + (0.01 × $500,000) divided by $500,000].

Since many factors influence the effective rate of a loan, when evaluating borrowing costs only the *effective annual rate* should be used as a standard of comparison to ensure that the actual costs of borrowing are used in making the decision.

To reduce their risks in making loans, banks may require collateral from borrowers. Collateral may be any asset that has value. If the borrower does not repay the loan, the bank owns the collateral and may sell it to recover the amount of the loan.

COLLATERAL

Typical collateral includes both specific high-value items owned by the company (such as buildings, computer equipment, or large machinery) and all items of a particular type (such as all raw materials or all inventory). Banks use blanket liens as collateral where individual items are of low value, but the collective value of all items is large enough to serve as collateral.

The highest level of risk comes in making loans to small companies, and it is not surprising to find that a high proportion of loans made to small companies—probably 75 percent—is secured. Larger companies present less risk and have stronger bargaining positions; only about 30 percent of loans made to companies in this class are secured. One aspect of protection that most banks require is *key person insurance* on the principal officers of the company taking out the loan. Since the repayment of the loan usually depends on the managers of the firm running the company in a profitable manner, if something should happen to a key manager, there may be some question about the safety of the loan. To avoid this uncertainty, a term insurance policy is taken out for the value of the loan on the life of the key manager. If he or she should die, the proceeds of the policy are paid to the bank in settlement of the loan.

When making loans to very small companies, banks often require that the owners and top managers personally sign for the loan also. Then, if the company does not repay the loan, the bank can claim the signer's personal assets, such as houses and stock investments.

To maximize the chances of success in applying for a bank loan, a company should carefully maintain good bank relations. Personal visits by the company president and other senior officers, as well as quarterly delivery

APPLYING FOR A BANK LOAN

of income statements, balance sheets, and cash flow statements, are useful means of sustaining such relations.

The actual process of obtaining bank credit (whether a line of credit or an actual loan) must be conducted on a personal basis with the bank loan officer. The loan officer will be interested in knowing how much money the company needs, how the company will use this money, how the company will repay the bank, and when the company will repay the bank. If you can fully answer these questions and support your answers with past results and realistic forecasts, you stand an excellent chance of obtaining the line of credit or loan you need.

One important item often overlooked in applying for bank credit is a cash forecast. Many financial managers prepare only projected income statements and balance sheets when they negotiate bank credit. Certainly, these projected financial statements are important, but as we have already seen, profits are not the same as cash, and the bank needs cash to be repaid. Therefore, a cash manager would do well to bring cash forecasts to the bank.

It might also be important to prepare more than one cash forecast. If time allows, you could prepare a cash forecast that assumes optimistically high sales and another that assumes pessimistically low sales. These forecasts will enable the banker (and you) to see the effects of unexpected financial changes and to determine the company's future cash requirements under several conditions.

➤ COMMERCIAL PAPER

Although many small and medium-sized companies must look to banks for short-term funds, many large corporations have the option of selling commercial paper. Commercial paper is an unsecured IOU from a large corporation to the buyer. Corporations sell the commercial paper either directly or through recognized dealers to other corporations, insurance companies, banks, money market funds, and pension funds. Commercial paper sells in denominations from $25,000 to several hundred million dollars. Maturities are always less than a year, usually between two and six months. In the last decade, the commercial paper market has undergone tremendous growth. Since 1977, the U.S. commercial paper market has grown from $50 billion to more than $350 billion and now exceeds the volume of traditional bank loans.

The interest rate for commercial paper falls between that of U.S. Treasury notes and the prime rate. Therefore, buyers willingly invest because they obtain a larger return than they could with Treasury notes. Similarly, corporations prefer selling commercial paper to taking out bank loans because they get their money at a lower cost. Recognized dealers in commercial paper typically charge 0.125 percent, which because of the large denominations involved, is large enough to compensate them for their services but small enough to keep the transactions attractive to both buyers and sellers.

The effective interest rate on commercial paper is determined by considering all of the issuing costs and interest costs. Issuing costs include any commitment fees paid for the back-up line of credit, the dealer's spread or underwriting fee, and other issuing costs. Interest costs, which are usually variable, are determined by calculating the actual cash flow paid to the investors in the commercial paper. The effective rate can be calculated by:

$$\text{Effective interest rate} = \frac{\text{Total costs}}{\text{Net proceeds}} \times \frac{365}{\text{Maturity}}$$

For example a $10 million face value commercial paper issue of Company ABC provides $9.95 million to the issuer. Financing costs are $1,000, and the interest rate paid is 8 percent per annum. The paper has a 180-day maturity. We can calculate the effective interest as:

$$\text{Effective interest rate} = \frac{1,000 + .08 \times 10,000,000 \times \frac{1}{2}}{9,950,000} \times \frac{365}{180}$$

$$= 8.17\%$$

Many corporations have another reason for preferring commercial paper to bank loans, namely, the ease with which commercial paper can be sold once the corporation has fully established its strength and reputation in the financial community. Instead of going through lengthy negotiations with its bank, the corporation can sell commercial paper quickly and easily through established channels. Today, corporations as a group sell almost half of their commercial paper on a direct basis with most of the direct paper being issued by finance companies. Through direct sales, a company avoids the charges of commercial paper dealers. Paper sold through dealers is usually issued by nonfinancial companies and smaller financial companies. These firms often lack the economies of scale needed to justify having a large staff to sell the paper.

➤ Accounts Receivable Financing

We have already seen how a company can convert its accounts receivable into cash more quickly through aggressive collection techniques. When a company fears that aggressive collection may offend customers and cause them to take their business to competitors, the company may decide to convert its accounts receivable to cash through a financing company. In this form of financing, the company can choose between two methods: pledging and factoring. In the following sections, we describe both methods. In practice, finance companies or banks offer many variations on these two financing methods.

Pledging means using accounts receivable as collateral for a loan from a finance company or bank. The finance company then gives money to the borrower and, as the borrower's customers pay their bills, the borrower repays the loan to the finance company.

Pledging

With this form of accounts receivable financing, the borrower's customers are not notified that their bills are being used as collateral for a loan. Therefore, pledging is called nonnotification financing. Furthermore, if customers do not pay their bills, the borrower (rather than the finance company) must absorb the loss. Thus, if the customer defaults, the lender has the right of recourse to the borrower.

In general, a finance company will not lend the full face value of the accounts receivable pledged. In determining what fraction of the face value of receivables to lend, the finance company considers three factors:

1. The credit rating of the borrower's customers (because bills that may be paid slowly, or not at all, obviously do not make good collateral).
2. The quantity and dollar value of the accounts receivable (because a small number of large dollar-value receivables is easier to control).
3. The borrower's credit rating (because the finance company prefers having the loan repaid to taking possession of the collateral).

Typically, a company can borrow 75 to 90 percent of the face value of its accounts receivable if it has a good credit rating and its customers have excellent credit ratings. Companies with lower credit ratings can generally borrow 60 to 75 percent of the face value of their receivables.

Pledging receivables is not a cheap source of credit. In recent years, when the commercial bank lending rate was between 8 and 15 percent, the cost of pledging receivables was almost 20 percent. Moreover, an additional charge is often made to cover the lender's expenses incurred in appraising credit risks. Therefore, this source of financing is used mostly by smaller companies that have no other source of funds open to them.

Another form of pledging is called pledging with notification, in which the borrower instructs its customers to pay their bills directly to the lender (often a bank). As checks from customers arrive, the bank deposits them in a special account and notifies the borrower that money has arrived.

PLEDGING WITH NOTIFICATION

With this approach, the lender controls the receivables more closely and does not have to worry that the borrower may collect pledged accounts receivable and then not notify the lender. The company loses under this system, however, because it must notify its customers that it has pledged its accounts receivable, which can reduce the company's credit rating.

Factoring is defined as selling an account receivable at a discount to a finance company, that is, to a factor. There are many variations of factoring, but the following example covers the major points. With factoring, a company usually transfers the functions of its credit department to the factor. That is, the factor takes over credit checking and collection. If the factor rejects a potential customer as an unacceptable credit risk, the company must either turn down the order or insist on cash payment.

FACTORING

Let's see how this process works in practice. Suppose Company B (buyer) orders $10,000 worth of material from Company S (seller). Company S calls its factor to report the order. The factor checks the credit rating of Company B and, if all is satisfactory, calls Company S with an approval. Company S then ships the goods and sends an invoice to Company B. The invoice instructs Company B to pay the factor.

At the same time, Company S sends a copy of the invoice to the factor, and the factor sends approximately 85 percent of the invoice amount ($8,500 in this case) to Company S. The factor must now collect the $10,000 from Company B. When the factor actually collects the bill, it may send Company S a small additional amount of money to recognize collections being higher than original estimates.

The fees that factors charge vary widely. These fees include an interest charge, usually expressed on a daily basis (for the time the bill is outstanding) and equivalent to a 15 to 30 percent annual interest rate; a collection fee, usually in the range of an additional 6 to 10 percent annual rate; and a credit checking charge, either a percentage of the invoice or a flat dollar amount. The factor keeps a hold-back amount (which is not immediately paid to Company S) to more than cover these various fees and charges. When Company B pays its bill, the factor computes all the relevant charges, deducts the total from the hold-back amount, and sends the remainder to Company S.

The effective cost of factoring can be calculated by the following:

$$\frac{\text{Effective annual}}{\text{factoring cost}} = \frac{\text{Total cost}}{\text{Funds available}} \times \frac{365}{\text{Number of days saved}}$$

For example, a company with monthly credit sales of $5 million has accounts receivable with an average maturity of 45 days. The factor charges a fee of 1 percent and the interest rate is 14 percent. If the company factors its accounts receivable, the number of days it takes from day of sale to cash inflow is reduced to 10 days. This means that instead of waiting (on average for 45 days) to realize the cash flow, the company gets the money in 10 days, for a saving of 35 days. Letting the factor process the accounts receivable saves the company $10,000 in expenses normally spent by the credit department. The effective cost of this arrangement is:

Effective annual factoring cost =

$$\frac{.14 \times 5,000,000 \times {}^{35}\!/_{365} + .01 \times 5,000,000 - 10,000}{5,000,000} \times \frac{365}{35}$$

$$= 22.3\%$$

Recourse

Factoring may be with or without recourse. In the previous example, factoring without recourse means that if Company B does not pay its bill, the factor must absorb the loss. Factoring with recourse, on the other hand, means that if Company B does not pay the bill within a prenegotiated time (for example, 90 days), the factor collects from Company S. Company S must then try to collect from Company B directly.

Naturally, a factor charges extra for factoring without recourse. Typically, a factor adds 6 to 12 percent (on an annual basis) to the interest rate it charges Company S. For factoring without recourse, factors generally come out ahead because they minimize bad-debt expense by carefully checking each customer's credit. Even so, Company S might prefer factoring without recourse for two reasons. First, Company S does not have to worry that any bills will be returned. In this way, factoring without recourse is a form of insurance. Second, the factor expresses the extra charge for factoring without recourse as part of the daily interest rate. This daily interest rate may look very small.

Most factoring is done with notification. This means that the customer company is notified and instructed to pay its bill directly to the factor. Sometimes factoring is done without notification. In this case, the customer sends its payment either directly to the supplier or to a post office box.

In general, factoring is more expensive than pledging. On the other hand, factors provide services, such as credit checking and collection, that a company would otherwise have to carry out itself.

➤ Loans Against Inventory

A company's inventory is an asset and can often be used as collateral for a loan. In this way, a company can get the cash it needs while still retaining access to its inventory. There are four basic ways to use inventory as security for a loan, depending on how closely the lender controls the physical inventory. These four ways are:

1. Chattel mortgage, in which specific inventory is used to secure the loan.
2. Floating (or blanket) lien, in which the loan is secured by all the borrower's inventory.
3. Field warehousing, in which the lender physically separates and guards the pledged inventory right on the borrower's premises.
4. Public warehousing, in which the lender transfers the pledged inventory to a separate warehouse.

A chattel (property) mortgage is a loan secured by specific assets. For example, a borrower might pledge 5,000 new refrigerators as collateral for a loan. To guarantee the lender's position as a secured creditor (in case of bankruptcy), a chattel mortgage must precisely describe the items pledged as collateral. In the case of the refrigerators, the loan agreement would include the serial numbers of the specific refrigerators pledged by the borrower. If the borrower sells some of these refrigerators or receives a new shipment of refrigerators, the chattel mortgage must be rewritten to include these changes specifically.

Because the chattel mortgage describes the collateral so specifically, it offers fairly high security to a lender. Lenders further reduce their risk by

Chattel Mortgage

lending only a fraction of the estimated market value of the collateral. This fraction depends on how easily the assets can be transported and sold. In the case of refrigerators, which are easy to sell, a borrower might obtain as much as 90 percent of their wholesale cost. But a borrower with a highly specialized inventory, such as bulldozer scoops, might get 50 percent or less of their fair market value because the lender would have difficulty selling the bulldozer scoops to recover the money. Because chattel mortgages describe the collateral so specifically, lenders limit their use to high-value items.

FLOATING LIEN

Instead of naming specific items of inventory to secure a loan, borrowers may pledge all of their inventory. This is a floating, or blanket, lien. Because such an arrangement does not describe specific items of inventory, it does not have to be rewritten each time the borrower sells an item from inventory or receives new items into inventory. However, this flexibility makes it extremely difficult for the lender to maintain the security for the loan. For example, the borrower might sell most of the inventory and not leave enough to secure the loan. For this reason, banks and finance companies will usually lend only a small fraction of the inventory's market value when using a floating lien.

FIELD WAREHOUSING

Field warehousing was invented to fully protect the lender's security. Under a field warehousing arrangement, the borrower designates a section of the premises, often a room or a specific area of the regular warehouse, for the use of the finance company. The finance company then locks and guards this field warehouse area and stores in it the actual inventory that the borrower is using as collateral. The finance company gives the borrower the agreed-on fraction of the fair market value of the inventory and receives in return a warehouse receipt, which gives the finance company title to the inventory. Companies use field warehousing when the inventory is especially bulky or valuable, such as structural steel, bulk chemicals, or diamonds.

Whenever the borrowing firm needs some of the inventory, it repays part of the loan, and the finance company releases part of the inventory. In this way, the finance company guarantees that there is sufficient collateral at all times to secure the loan.

PUBLIC WAREHOUSING

Public warehousing is similar to field warehousing except that the actual inventory is moved to an independent warehouse away from the borrower's plant. As with field warehousing, the finance company releases inventory as the borrower repays the loan. Again, this ensures that the collateral is always sufficient to cover the loan.

There are many variations of warehousing. For example, some bonded warehouses accept checks in payment for loans and then forward these checks to the finance company while releasing the appropriate amount of inventory to the borrower. If such an arrangement is acceptable to all parties, it helps the borrower regain title to the inventory more quickly.

Warehousing companies collect both a service charge and interest. The service charge is usually a fixed amount plus 1 to 2 percent of the loan itself. This service charge covers the cost of providing field warehousing facilities or of transferring inventory to a public warehouse. In addition, the warehouse company charges interest, usually 10 percent or more. Because of the high fixed costs of setting up a warehousing system, this form of financing is practical only for inventories larger than about $500,000.

COSTS OF WAREHOUSING

➤ CUSTOMER PREPAYMENTS

Some companies are actually financed by their customers. This situation typically occurs on large, complex, long-term projects; it includes defense contractors, building contractors, ship builders, and management consulting firms. These companies typically divide their large projects into a series of stages and require payment as they complete each stage. This significantly reduces the cash these companies require, compared to firms that finance an entire project themselves and receive payment on completion. In some companies, customers pay in advance for everything they buy. Many mail-order operations are financed this way.

➤ CHOOSING THE RIGHT MIX
OF SHORT-TERM FINANCING

The financial manager is interested in securing the required short-term funds at the lowest cost. The lowest cost usually results from some combination of trade credit, unsecured and secured bank loans, accounts receivable financing, and inventory financing. Though it is virtually impossible to evaluate every possible combination of short-term financing, financial managers can use their experience and subjective opinion to put together a short-term financing package that will have a reasonable cost. At the same time, the manager must be aware of future requirements and of the impact that using certain sources today may have on the availability of short-term funds in the future.

In selecting the best financing package, the cash manager should consider the firm's current situation and requirements, the current and future costs of the alternatives, and the firm's future situation and requirements. For small firms, the options available may be somewhat limited, and the total short-term financing package may be less important. On the other hand, larger firms may be faced with a myriad of possibilities. Clearly, the short-term borrowing decision can become quite complex, but the selection of the right combination can be of significant financial value to the cash manager's firm.

➤ **SUMMARY**

In this chapter, we looked at the many ways companies obtain short-term cash. Companies should first be sure they are collecting from their customers as quickly as competitive conditions allow and, simultaneously, paying their suppliers as slowly as practical. Companies often look next to banks for short-term cash. A company can establish a line of credit first and then borrow against it. The most common bank loan is for 90 days, is unsecured, and carries an interest rate that ranges from the prime rate to about 3 percent over prime, depending on the financial strength of the borrower. Larger companies can borrow directly from other companies, banks, or individuals by selling commercial paper. Companies can also use their assets to get cash. They can pledge their receivables as collateral for a loan, or they can sell the receivables (at a discount) to a finance company. Similarly, a company can use its inventory as collateral for a loan.

CHAPTER 8

LEASE-VERSUS-BUY DECISIONS

By the end of this chapter, the reader will be able to:

1. Define and compare an operating lease and a financial lease.
2. Explain the advantages and disadvantages of leasing versus buying.
3. Perform a lease-versus-buy analysis and select the best alternative.
4. Evaluate a lease arrangement from the perspective of the lessor.

In this chapter, we discuss leasing and the way it fits into a corporate cash management program. We first describe what a lease is and examine the issue of use versus ownership. In addition, we discuss the tax and nontax attributes associated with leasing. For example, we address flexibility, obsolescence, convenience, economies of scale, and off-balance-sheet financing. Moreover, we provide examples of how to analyze a lease-versus-buy decision from both the lessee's and lessor's perspective.

➤ DEFINITION OF

A LEASE

A lease is a contract under which the lessee (user) gains the use of an asset from the lessor (owner) in return for committing himself or herself to a series of periodic payments over the term of the lease. The key factor of a lease arrangement is the separation of use from ownership. The analysis that we look at in this chapter does not determine whether or not the investments should be accepted or rejected. We assume the investment proposal has already undergone analysis and has been accepted. Given the decision to accept the investment proposal, the next issue is financing the acquisition. Should we lease the asset or buy it? In this chapter, we provide an analysis of the decision to finance an acceptable investment proposal by either leasing the asset or borrowing money to purchase it. Exhibit 8–1 graphically illustrates the distinction between leasing and buying.

As this exhibit illustrates, under a buying arrangement the using firm must raise sufficient capital from internal sources or resort to issuing bonds

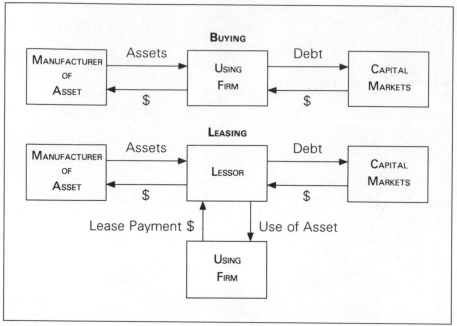

Exhibit 8–1   Leasing as Distinguished from Buying

to the capital market, using its own credit standing, to purchase the investment. One problem with this approach is that the firm may not have the credit needed to get the best rates in the capital market. An alternative would be for a major financial institution, with a good credit rating, to raise the necessary funds in the capital market, use the funds to purchase an asset, and then lease it to the firm. Under this scenario, the cost of financing is reduced, and the firm acquires the use of the asset while the financial institution shares in the financing cost saving. Everyone is satisfied—the firm uses the asset, the financial institution earns a fee, and the capital market receives a high-rated security. Additionally, the using company is faced with a much smaller cash outflow spread over a number of years under the leasing alternative.

➤ Types of Leases

Although there are several types of leases, they usually fall into one of two general categories: operating leases and financial leases.

Operating Leases

Operating leases are characterized as short-term leases with a cancellation clause and maintenance and service generally provided by the lessor (owner of the asset). The short-term nature of operating leases implies that the lessor makes money only through additional extensions of the lease contract or through asset disposition at an attractive price. However, the cancellation clause enables the lessee (user of the asset) to cancel the lease agreement prior to the expiration of the lease term. This in effect shifts the risks of equipment obsolescence to the lessor. Some products, such as computer equipment, may have a high level of obsolescence risk because of the changing technology within the industry. Consequently, the lessor needs to factor these risks in the price of the lease contract. One way the lessor might earn additional funds is through a service and maintenance contract. Though the lessor usually provides these services for the lessee, they are not without cost. The cost is usually impounded in the lease agreement or a separate contract is signed to cover this arrangement.

FINANCIAL LEASES

Financial, or capital, leases generally contain lease terms much longer than those of operating leases. Moreover, financial leases typically cover the complete life of the underlying asset and as such do not provide a cancellation clause. In effect, the lessee acts as the owner of the asset. Thus, the lessee makes individual arrangements to provide servicing and maintenance and will probably also pay for insurance and property taxes. Renewable options may be provided by the lessor, but these are subject to scrutiny by the Internal Revenue Service.

SALE AND LEASEBACK

A unique form of financial lease, the sale and leaseback, is created when the asset already owned by a firm is sold to a lessor and then leased back by the original owner. The lessee in essence is refinancing the property with a lessor (typically a financial institution) and freeing up cash flow to invest in other areas. The lessor in return receives a series of payments that provide not only a return of capital but presumably a reasonable return on interest as well.

➤ WHY IS LEASING SO POPULAR?

Leasing has become popular in recent years because there has been a trend emphasizing the ability to use property over the legal ownership of property. Other reasons often mentioned include the sharing of tax benefits between lessors and lessees. But the big incentive for leasing continues to be the nontax attributes such as flexibility, a hedge against obsolescence and inflation risk, service and maintenance contracts, convenience, lower costs, and off-balance-sheet financing.

➤ USE VERSUS OWNERSHIP

Many businesspeople have come to realize that the use of a piece of equipment is more important to the production of income than the possession of a piece of paper conveying title to the equipment. In fact, if people can use equipment for most of its economic life without having the full legal responsibilities, risks, and burdens of ownership, why should they ever desire to own it? Even farmers, who may have traditionally valued land ownership, now readily acknowledge that the use of land is more important than *ownership* of it. Many farmers and ranchers lease tracts of land to increase production of cattle or crops.

A big boost to leasing over the years has been the sharing of large tax benefits created through accelerated depreciation and investment tax writeoffs. Lessees in low or negative tax positions were not able to enjoy the full tax benefits of asset ownership. Lessors in high tax positions, however, could share some of the tax benefits through competitive lease pricing. **Tax Considerations**

In 1981, Congress enacted the Economic Recovery Tax Act (ERTA), which significantly increased the tax benefits by means of the Accelerated Cost Recovery System (ACRS) and by shortening the recovery period for the Investment Tax Credit (ITC). ERTA also introduced safe-harbor leasing, which liberalized the provisions of leasing by removing stringent profit-motive standards. With safe-harbor leasing, lessors and lessees could engage in a transaction motivated by a pure tax benefit transfer. Prior legislation ruled this illegal.

Since 1981, every major tax bill has included provisions that remove some of the tax incentives created through leasing. The Tax Equity Fiscal Responsibility Act of 1982 (TEFRA) repealed the safe-harbor rules for ERTA and established "finance lease" rules, which mandate that leases need to have a substantive economic purpose other than tax benefit transfers. The Deficit Reduction Act (DRA) of 1984 further modified some of the tax rules by changing the ITC and reducing some of the depreciation available on property leased to tax-exempt entities. The Tax Reform Act of 1986 had a major impact on equipment leasing since the bill eliminated the ITC, modified the depreciation allowances, lowered the corporate tax rates, and increased the corporate minimum tax. The first three concerns all reduced the tax benefits associated with equipment ownership, and the corporate minimum tax restricted the capacity of lessors to engage in tax-related transactions. However, leasing still enjoys some tax advantages for certain type of companies.

Although in the past leasing may have gained from the investment credit and other tax benefits, it doesn't depend on the tax code for its survival. Much of the growth in leasing of late has been a result of nontax attributes. Many lease and tax experts generally agree that some companies, especially nonfinancial companies that did leveraged leasing primarily for the tax advantage, will leave the market. They also point out that a principal purpose of leasing is asset use, not ownership. **Nontax Attributes**

Leasing provides 100 percent financing, flexibility in usage requirements and terms, fixed rates, and convenience. Furthermore, from the lessee's perspective, leasing is a source of off-balance-sheet financing, a hedge against obsolescence and inflation risks, and often a cheaper financing source than borrowing. These attributes are particularly useful to lessees, which are often cash-poor companies.

Flexibility is a major factor in the recent growth of leasing. A short-term cancelable lease offers a firm flexibility, particularly if the leased asset is in an industry undergoing rapid technological advances. If a superior product comes to market, the lessee can cancel the current lease and enter into a new lease with the new product. Many managers mention the ability to specifically structure the financial and usage terms of the lease agreement as one of the major benefits of leasing.

In addition to allowing flexibility provisions, leases seldom contain the restrictive covenants usually found in loan agreements. Some loan agreements, for example, prohibit future financing of equipment until the loan is paid down significantly; leasing allows further expansion without restrictions.

FLEXIBILITY OF LEASES

Another reason use of equipment has been emphasized is that penalties are attached to the ownership of equipment, such as computers, developed by high-technology industries undergoing rapid growth. Some computers have even become obsolete between the order date and the delivery date—and who wants to own an outmoded piece of equipment? Short-term, cancelable leases permit firms to avoid the pitfalls of owning obsolete equipment. If a piece of equipment becomes outdated, the lessee cancels the lease and orders updated equipment. In fact, automatic replacement of obsolete equipment is written into an upgrade lease agreement. A renewable operating lease enables a lessee to transfer the obsolescence risk to the lessor, who presumably is in a better position to resell a product and to forecast the residual value of a piece of equipment. Some lessors, such as Equitable Life Leasing, even specialize in equipment where the risk of technological obsolescence is great.

OBSOLESCENCE OF EQUIPMENT

Some lessees are attracted to leasing because of lower costs, fewer down-payment restrictions, and convenience. Leasing companies generally require down payments lower than other financial institutions. The typical lease requires the first and last rental payments in advance (representing 2 to 4 percent down), whereas many banks require 10 to 20 percent as a down payment. In addition, other incidental costs of acquiring the asset, such as sales tax and installation charges, can be included as part of the lease payments rather than (as required by other financial institutions) paid in advance along with the large down payment. Frequently, the opportunity cost of tying up cash in equipment acquisitions is high enough that it almost necessitates leasing as an alternative. This is especially true for rapidly growing companies, where available funds are tied up in accounts receivable and inventory. (For example, if a small, growing firm needs a piece of equipment that it cannot afford to buy from funds generated internally, it may be able to lease the equipment immediately.)

COST AND CONVENIENCE

Compared to conventional equipment financing, with its large down payments and short-term payouts, leasing may offer a hedge against inflation.

LEASING AS AN INFLATION HEDGE

The longer terms and lower down payments generally available in leases may allow the lessee to make future lease payments with inflated dollars. The lessor can obtain protection from inflation as well by borrowing long term and passing this protection on to the lessee in the form of equal lease payments over a long term. Generally, it is better to borrow long term in a period of inflation, assuming one's revenue sources are expected to inflate correspondingly and assuming future inflation is not already built into the borrowing rate or lease price.

ECONOMIES OF SCALE

Certain leasing companies, because of their large size, can effect savings in the form of quantity discounts received from volume purchasing. Such savings can be partially passed on to the lessee. Additional savings from economies of scale may be obtained through the *service lease*, in which the cost of maintaining the leased equipment is included as part of each rental payment.

Autos, trucks, computers, and office copiers are examples of equipment often accompanied by a maintenance and service contract. Many lessees believe that leasing companies, because of familiarity with the equipment and large size, may be more proficient in servicing the equipment and will therefore pass along any savings. It does not always follow that large size and efficiency go hand in hand, however. Therefore, savings must be ascertained by comparing lease rates charged by competing companies.

Large leasing companies usually have access to secondary markets in which returned equipment may be resold. Since operating leases tend to be short term, a great reliance is placed on the resale or salvage value. Lessors assume the risk of the resale value and are often willing to wait until the end of the lease term to realize their return objective. Thus, they are able to reduce their front-end cost to the lessee and may charge a lower lease payment.

OFF-BALANCE-SHEET FINANCING

Operating leases that meet certain accounting criteria are not capitalized on the balance sheet of the lessee. Thus, the lessee can acquire the use of equipment without showing the lease as a payable liability on its balance sheet. This attribute is not as significant as it once was owing to stricter reporting requirements and more sophisticated creditors. However, some creditors may not consider leases as debt if they are properly structured. This may enlarge the firm's overall debt capacity.

➤ LEASE-VERSUS-BUY
ANALYSIS

The best way to compare the effects of leasing and acquisition on debt financing is to calculate the after-tax cash flows under each alternative and find the difference in the present value of these cash flows. To calculate the advantage of leasing, we identify all the relevant cash flows attributable to leasing—that is, those cash flows that will be different if leasing rather than owning is selected. By leasing, the firm avoids the cash outlay required to purchase the asset, incurs an obligation to make lease payments, forgoes the depreciation tax shield, and forgoes the residual value of the asset at the end of the lease. The costs of operation, maintenance, insurance, and property taxes also affect the after-tax cash flow and must be included. Exhibit 8–2 presents a lease-versus-buy cash flow analysis.

In this exhibit, the formula for calculating the leasing cash flows appears first, with explanations of each term below. Next the formula for calculating the buying cash flows is given, again with explanations below. The leasing equation states that the net present value (NPV) is a function of an initial leasing outflow (net of tax) minus the annual operating costs (net of tax). In other words, it is looking at the total cost of leasing in today's dollar. The NPV of buying is looking at the total cost of buying an asset in today's dollars. Each of these approaches discounts the cash flows at a previously determined cost of capital rate. The cost of capital rate recognizes that today's cash flows are worth more than the same cash flows in five or ten years. This is why all cash flows are discounted back at some cost of capital rate (the rate varies from firm to firm) and expressed in today's dollars. The next to last column in Exhibit 8–3 shows the present value (PV) rate for cash flows discounted at 10 percent. For instance, a cash flow one year from now is worth only (.909 × cash flow) in today's dollars. A cash flow five years from now is worth only (.621 × cash flow) in today's dollars.

The buying approach equation in Exhibit 8–2 shows that the cost of buying an asset is a series of cash inflows and outflows. The equation begins by looking at the initial cost of the asset as a negative outflow plus the annual inflow of depreciation benefits (adjusted for taxes) minus the annual operating costs outflow (adjusted for taxes) plus the residual value inflow of the asset on disposition. Depreciation and residual values are recognized as positive cash flow inflows because depreciation reduces taxable income and thus reduces tax outflows, and the sale of the asset at its residual value creates a cash inflow and return of the initial investment.

The equation below the buying equation is the net advantage to leasing (NAL). This equation simply states that the benefit to leasing is the difference between the total costs of leasing (in today's dollars) minus the total cost of buying (in today's dollars). When the NAL is positive (that is, greater than zero), the asset should be leased; when the NAL is negative, the firm will maximize its cash flows by buying the assets.

If we apply the analysis to the following situation, we can determine the desirability of leasing compared to buying. Company MNO, with a cost of capital of 10 percent, has the opportunity to purchase an asset for $100,000. The same asset can be leased for five years with an annual lease payment of $30,000 per year. If the asset is purchased, operating expenses will be $15,000 per year; if it is leased, they will be $14,000 per year. The asset will be depreciated under the modified Accelerated Cost Recovery System (ACRS) schedule at the rates given for a five-year property. We assume the half-year convention, and therefore the final half year of depreciation is taken in the sixth year. Assume the after-tax cash inflow from

LEASING

$$NPV = -\text{Lease payment} \times (1 - \text{Tax rate}) - \text{Operating costs} \times (1 - \text{Tax rate})$$
$$\qquad\qquad\qquad\qquad\qquad (\text{Yearly cash flows}) \qquad\qquad\qquad (\text{Yearly cash flows})$$

BUYING

$$NPV = -\text{Cost of asset} + (\text{Depreciation} \times \text{Tax rate}) - \text{Operating costs} \times (1 - \text{Tax rate}) + \text{Residual after-tax value}$$
$$\qquad (\text{Cash flow year 0}) \qquad\qquad (\text{Yearly cash flows}) \qquad\qquad (\text{Yearly cash flows}) \qquad\qquad (\text{Cash flow year } n)$$

NET ADVANTAGE OF LEASING OVER BUYING

$$NAL = \text{Leasing cash flows} - \text{Buying cash flows}$$

$$NAL = +\frac{COST}{(1+K)^0} - \sum_{t=1}^{n} \frac{D_t T}{(1+K)^t} + \sum_{t=1}^{n} \frac{(OC_B - OC_L) \times (1 - T)}{(1+K)^t} - \frac{R_n}{(1+K)^n} - \sum_{t=1}^{n} \frac{L_t(1 - T)}{(1+K)^t}$$

DECISION:

NAL>0 signifies leasing is preferred.
NAL≤0 signifies buying is preferred.

Note: K = Discount rate (or firm's cost of capital)

EXHIBIT 8–2   LEASE-VERSUS-BUY CASH FLOW ANALYSIS

the sale of the asset at the end of five years will be zero. At present, the company has a marginal tax rate of 34 percent that is expected to remain the same for the next five years. This situation is analyzed in Exhibit 8–3.

In the case depicted, the best way of financing the acquisition is to lease the asset. If we look at the components of the NAL, we can see why this is true. On a present-value after-tax basis, buying the asset requires a cash outflow of $100,000, whereas leasing the asset requires a present value of lease payments of $75,042. So far, leasing is cheaper by $24,958. Since the operating costs of the lease are cheaper than the operating costs of buying by $2,052, leasing now has an advantage of $27,460. Finally, the depreciation tax benefit of purchasing the asset has a present value of $26,299. This makes the NAL $1,161 in favor of leasing. Hence, because the NAL is positive, leasing is the better form of financing here.

➤ THE LESSOR'S VIEWPOINT

The discussion so far has been limited to the case of the lessee. The capital budgeting framework is also appropriate to use in evaluating the lessor's investment in a lease arrangement. Both the lessor and the lessee are interested in the results of the analysis. The lessor is concerned with earning a reasonable return on invested capital. And the lessee is interested in how much the lessor is earning on a given lease arrangement because, in most cases, the terms of the lease are negotiable. If the lessor is earning too high a profit, the lessee may be able to negotiate a more favorable arrangement.

From the lessor's perspective, we need to determine the initial cash outlay for the asset and any advances made by the lessee. The cash inflows consist of the after-tax lease payments adjusted for operating expenses, including depreciation, maintenance, property taxes, and any after-tax residual value the asset may have when the lease expires. If the cash inflows (benefits) exceed the initial outlay (costs), the leasing arrangement can be considered. Otherwise, the terms of the lease may have to be modified to make the lease more attractive to the lessor.

If we assume that the lessor is a corporation in the 34 percent tax bracket and that an alternative investment in bonds offers an after-tax return of 8 percent, would this company enter into a five-year lease arrangement for an asset that costs $100,000? The lease payment would be $25,500 per year. Exhibit 8–4 illustrates how the lease arrangement could be analyzed from the point of view of the lessor.

In this exhibit, we see that the lessor is receiving cash inflows of $25,500 (from lease revenue) and is experiencing cash outflows resulting from operating costs and income taxes. The income tax burden is calculated in the top section of Exhibit 8–4 and reflects the firm's revenue minus depreciation expenses and operating costs. The annual tax burden is $1,530, –$2,550, $1,870, $4,250, $4,250, and –$1,700. In years 2 and 6, the firm has a tax loss that results in a tax refund.

The lessor's annual cash flow per year is determined by simply adding the annual cash inflows and subtracting the annual cash outflows. The

BUYING
Depreciation

Year	Depreciation[a]	Tax Rate	(Cost)/Savings	PV Rate	PV[b]
1	$20,000	.34	$ 6,800	.909	$ 6,181
2	32,000	.34	10,880	.826	8,987
3	19,000	.34	6,460	.751	4,851
4	12,000	.34	4,080	.683	2,787
5	12,000	.34	4,080	.621	2,534
6	5,000	.34	1,700	.564	959
Net (cost) savings					$26,299

Operating Costs

Year	Cost	Tax Benefit (34%)	Net Cost	PV Rate	PV
1	$15,000	$ 5,100	$ 9,900	.909	$ 8,999
2	15,000	5,100	9,900	.826	8,177
3	15,000	5,100	9,900	.751	7,435
4	15,000	5,100	9,900	.683	6,762
5	15,000	5,100	9,900	.621	6,148
					$37,521
Salvage value of asset at end of useful life					$ 0

LEASING
Lease Payments

Year	Lease Payment	Tax Savings (34%)	Net Cost	PV Rate	PV
1	$30,000	$10,200	$19,800	.909	$17,998
2	30,000	10,200	19,800	.826	16,355
3	30,000	10,200	19,800	.751	14,870
4	30,000	10,200	19,800	.683	13,523
5	30,000	10,200	19,800	.621	12,296
Total lease payments					$75,042

Operating Costs

Year	Cost	Tax Benefit (34%)	Net Cost	PV Rate	PV
1	$14,000	$ 4,760	$ 9,240	.909	$ 8,399
2	14,000	4,760	9,240	.826	7,632
3	14,000	4,760	9,240	.751	6,939
4	14,000	4,760	9,240	.683	6,311
5	14,000	4,760	9,240	.621	5,738
					$35,019

NAL = Cost − Depreciation benefit + Operating cost savings[c] − Sales value − Lease cost
= $100,000 − $26,299 + $2,502 − 0 − $75,042 = $1,161

Decision: Leasing is better.

[a]Depreciation basis is $100,000; depreciation rates are 20, 32, 19, 12, 12, and 5%, respectively.
[b]PV implies present value.
[c]The present value of operating costs of buying ($37,521) less the present value of operating costs of leasing ($35,019).

Exhibit 8–3   Lease-Versus-Buy Analysis for Company MNO

inflows consist of lease revenues of $25,500 for the first five years plus tax refunds of $2,550 and $1,700 for years 2 and 6, respectively. The outflows consist of operating costs of $1,000 per year assumed by the lessor and income taxes of $1,530, $1,870, $4,250, and $4,250 paid in years 1, 3, 4, and 5, respectively. The decision to lease or not lease is now a function of discounting the cash flows to reflect the different timing of inflows and outflows. The lessor has an initial cash outflow of $100,000 for the purchase of the asset. In return, the lessor receives annual cash inflows of $22,970, $27,050, $22,630, $20,250, $20,250, and $1,700 over the next six years. To assess the cash flows in today's dollars, the future cash flows (years 1–6) are discounted at an assumed opportunity cost of 8 percent (hypothetical benchmark return). After adding the discounted cash inflows and subtracting the initial $100,000 outlay, the firm is left with a net present value (NPV) of –$7,835. A negative NPV implies that the future cash inflows are not large enough to offset the $100,000 outlay and that consequently the lessor would not generate a return of 8 percent (the discount rate). As a result, the firm (assuming it demands a return of at least 8 percent) would reject this project and decide not to lease.

Given that the lessor should reject the proposed lease arrangement based on the analysis shown in Exhibit 8–4, is there anything that can be done to restructure the lease so that it becomes acceptable? Various kinds of changes can be made: The term of the lease could be lengthened or shortened, the lease payment could be increased, or the expenses associated with operating costs could be reassessed. For simplicity, we assume that the corporation decides to increase the lease payment and keep everything else the same.

> ## SUMMARY

Managing corporate cash requires analysis of long- and short-term cash flows. In earlier chapters, we look at the flows of cash resulting from normal working capital management. In this chapter, we examined a longer-term approach to cash flow management of fixed assets. When examining long-term projects, the financial manager needs to make important decisions about the financing of major assets. One obvious choice is to purchase the desired asset with either corporate cash or borrowed funds; an alternative is leasing.

In this chapter, we discussed leasing and the analysis of lease arrangements from the perspective of both the user and the owner of the asset (the lessee and the lessor). We spoke of the advantages and disadvantages of leasing and presented several models to analyze the cash flows associated with the leasing transaction. We also introduced an NAL (net advantage to leasing) analytical framework for evaluating the lease arrangements from the perspective of the lessee. Furthermore, we presented an NPV (net present value) approach for the lessor to use in deciding whether or not to engage in a leasing transaction. Finally, we provided an analysis of the lease-versus-buy transaction.

Term of lease = 5 years
Alternative investment yield = 8% (K)
Cash outflow
   Cost of equipment $100,000
   Residual after-tax value   0

ANNUAL TAX BURDEN

	YEAR 1	YEAR 2	YEAR 3	YEAR 4	YEAR 5	YEAR 6
Lease revenue	$25,500	$25,500	$25,500	$25,500	$25,500	—
Less						
Depreciation	20,000	32,000	19,000	12,000	12,000	$5,000
Operating costs	1,000	1,000	1,000	1,000	1,000	—
Taxable income	4,500	−7,500	5,500	12,500	12,500	—
Tax at 34%	$1,530	−$2,550	$1,870	$4,250	$4,250	−$1,700

ANNUAL CASH FLOW PER YEAR

	YEAR 1	YEAR 2	YEAR 3	YEAR 4	YEAR 5	YEAR 6
Lease revenue	$25,500	$25,500	$25,500	$25,500	$25,500	—
Less						
Operating costs	1,000	1,000	1,000	1,000	1,000	—
Income taxes	1,530	−2,550	1,870	4,250	4,250	−1,700
Total cash flow	$22,970	$27,050	$22,630	$20,250	$20,250	$1,700

$$NPV = -\text{COST} + \sum_{t=1}^{n=5} \frac{\text{CASH FLOW}}{(1 + K)^t}$$

$$NPV = \$100,000 + \frac{\$22,970}{(1.08)^1} + \frac{\$27,050}{(1.08)^2} + \frac{\$22,630}{(1.08)^3} + \frac{\$20,250}{(1.08)^4} + \frac{\$20,250}{(1.08)^5} + \frac{\$1,700}{(1.08)^6}$$

$$= -\$100,000 + \$22,970(.926) + \$27,050(.857)$$
$$+ \$22,630(.794) + \$20,250(.735) + \$20,250(.681) + \$1,700(.630)$$

$$= -\$100,000 + \$21,270 + \$23,182 + \$17,968 + \$14,884 + \$13,790 + \$1,071$$

$$NPV = -\$7,835$$

DECISION: DO NOT LEASE.

EXHIBIT 8–4   ANALYZING A PROPOSED LEASE AGREEMENT

   Although this chapter presented only an overview of a complex topic, it did provide you with ideas for future project financing. Leasing is designed to be a flexible financing vehicle. This may someday be helpful to the corporate cash manager who anticipates future problems and presents alternative and flexible strategies.

CHAPTER 9

INVESTING SURPLUS CASH

By the end of this chapter, the reader will be able to:

1. List the sources of surplus cash available for investment.
2. Describe the four criteria for investing surplus cash.
3. Discuss the investment characteristics of various types of marketable securities.
4. Describe the features of adjustable rate preferred stock and Dutch Auction rate preferred stock.

LEARNING OBJECTIVES

Very often, a corporation has surplus cash that it does not need for its immediate business activities. If the corporation leaves this surplus cash in its checking account, it earns no return or a very small return. For this reason, corporations try to invest their surplus cash so that they can earn interest. In this chapter, we describe the many ways corporations earn money with their surplus cash.

➤ SOURCES OF SURPLUS CASH

Corporate cash managers frequently find that they have surplus cash available for investment. This cash may come from any of several sources:

1. *Following a seasonal sales peak.* If a company's strongest selling season is summer and its customers pay within 30 to 60 days, the company is likely to have surplus cash in the fall.
2. *After receiving the proceeds from a large loan.* Frequently, companies negotiate bank loans for more than their immediate needs. For example, if a company sees that it will need $600,000 over the next six months for inventory buildup, it may borrow the entire amount at the beginning of the period instead of borrowing $100,000 each month. This simplifies bank negotiations, but it leaves the company with surplus cash that it must invest profitably to offset bank interest charges.

3. *After leasing equipment.* A company may decide to lease equipment that it had planned to buy, or the company might sell an existing piece of equipment to a leasing company and then lease it back. Either way, the company will find itself with surplus cash.
4. *Following the sale of stock or the placement of bonds.* A company may raise money by selling additional shares of its own stock or by placing its bonds with outside investors. Either way, the company probably will be unable to use the sudden influx of cash immediately and must invest the surplus cash.

In addition to these situations, a company may have surplus cash simply from its day-to-day activities. For example, if several large customers pay sooner than expected, the company may have $2 million a week earlier than it had planned. An efficient cash manager can profitably invest this extra money for one week.

Very often, a company may have surplus cash at the same time that it owes money to banks or has bonds outstanding. Why not simply pay back the bank? Sometimes this is the correct thing to do, but more often the company's cash surplus is temporary, and the cash manager should look for a temporary investment. If a company prepaid part of its bank loan with temporary surplus cash, the company might have to go back to the bank for an additional loan in a week or two.

➤ Guidelines for Investing Surplus Cash

Cash managers use four criteria when they invest surplus cash. These guidelines are:

1. *Safety.* The first responsibility of cash managers is to prevent the loss of capital. They must analyze each investment in terms of the risk of default by the borrower; they must carefully assess the probability that the borrower will pay all contracted interest and repay the principal at maturity. In the case of marketable securities, cash managers must also assess the risk of a drop in the market value of the security.
2. *Liquidity.* Liquidity refers to how quickly the company can convert its investment back into cash. Many marketable securities can be changed back to cash overnight. Other investments require anywhere from a few days to 90 days. In general, the cash manager must either select very liquid (quickly convertible) investments or match the maturity of investments to the company's needs. For example, if a company has surplus cash that it will need in 30 days to make a lease down payment, the cash manager may give preference to an investment that matures in 30 days.
3. *Return.* The cash manager must look at the return—or profit—that each potential investment offers. To calculate the return accurately, the cash manager must include such expenses as commissions to brokers and handling time by the company.

4. *Taxability*. Finally, the cash manager must assess the taxability of each investment. Some investments offer a lower apparent return, but the income from them is taxed at a lower rate so that the after-tax return is fully competitive with other investments.

➤ BANK ACCOUNTS

Most corporations hold some of their funds in a demand deposit in a commercial bank. These funds are immediately available, but the bank is not permitted to pay interest on *corporate* demand deposits. An alternative to the demand deposit is a time deposit. In exchange for a return, the corporation must be willing to give up immediate availability of funds that demand deposits offer. Time deposit accounts are safe up to a certain amount because they are insured by the Federal Deposit Insurance Corporation (FDIC), just like demand deposits.

There are several types of time deposits. Regular savings accounts are used predominately by individuals and small corporations. Bank savings accounts do not usually offer a high return; in fact, the interest they are allowed to offer is limited by law. In addition, many banks are not chartered to offer interest-paying savings accounts to corporations. The maturity of savings accounts is indefinite. You can keep the money in the account for as long or as short a time as you want.

Another type of time account is the certificate of deposit (CD). CDs are the interest-paying obligations of commercial banks. The two major differences between the CD and a regular savings account are maturity and amount of interest. The maturity of a CD is fixed, and the rate of interest at the point of inception can vary.

➤ MARKETABLE SECURITIES

Although cash managers may hold some surplus cash in a bank savings account, most cash managers prefer to earn a significantly higher return by investing in some of the many types of marketable securities. To select the appropriate mix of marketable securities, a cash manager should first divide the available surplus funds into three classifications. These classifications are:

1. *Backup cash*. A company may need extra cash quickly. Therefore, a portion of the surplus funds should be invested in securities that are readily converted into cash, that is, securities with high liquidity.
2. *Predictable cash needs*. A company can predict many of its cash needs. Thus, some surplus cash can be invested in securities with longer maturities that will yield cash for such predictable needs as payroll, taxes, and dividends.
3. *Free cash*. Once a company has provided for emergency backup needs and predictable needs, its remaining cash is free. Since the securities in this part of a company's portfolio are not earmarked for any specific or immediate purpose, the cash manager is able to invest these funds in securities offering a higher return. Short-term liquidity is not so important for these investments.

The most important factor in deciding which securities you should buy for each segment is the liquidity of the investment. Obviously, the cash backup segment of the portfolio must be instantly convertible into cash. Securities bought for predicted cash needs should ideally have maturities that closely match the cash requirement dates. And, finally, securities in the free cash segment of the portfolio may mature in any reasonable time. Importance of Liquidity

Going back to the four guidelines for investing surplus cash—safety, liquidity, return, and taxability—we can now outline the three-step process for selecting marketable securities. First, every security must offer a high degree of safety, or you must discard it from further consideration. Second, you should match the liquidity (or maturity) of each security to its purpose (cash backup, specific need, or free investment). Third, within the constraints of safety and liquidity, you should seek the securities offering the highest return (remembering, of course, to consider commissions, handling time, and taxes). Selection Process

There are nine important types of marketable securities: U.S. Treasury bills, federal agency issues, commercial paper, certificates of deposit, banker's acceptances, repurchase agreements, tax-exempt obligations, money market funds, and Eurodollar deposits. Exhibit 9–1 summarizes the nine types, and we discuss them more fully in the following sections. Types of Marketable Securities

U.S. TREASURY SECURITIES

U.S. Treasury securities account for the largest fraction of the money market. The Treasury issues several forms of securities, including Treasury bills, tax anticipation bills, notes, and bonds.

Treasury bills (T-bills) are extremely popular because of their safety, high trading volume, and variety of maturities. T-bills are considered completely safe because they are backed by the U.S. government. However, the bills are traded on the open market, and if you sell them before maturity, you may suffer from temporary market fluctuations. The Treasury auctions its T-bills weekly and offers standard maturities of 91 days and 182 days. Subsequently, these T-bills are traded in a broad secondary market handled by registered security dealers and banks. Because of this broad secondary market and the weekly auctions, you can purchase T-bills that mature almost any week that you want during the coming year. The Treasury sells its three-month and six-month bills every week; in addition, it periodically sells nine-month and one-year bills.

T-bills do not pay interest as such. Instead, they are sold at a discount from the par or face value. The holder then collects the full face value at maturity and, in this way, earns a return on his or her investment. For example, a 91-day T-bill might sell for $98.50. That is, you buy the T-bill now for $98.50, and you will receive $100.00 in 91 days. This $1.50 profit for 91 days (one-fourth of a year) is roughly equivalent to $6.00 annually, or 6 percent.

Investment	Description	Denominations	Safety	Maturity	Liquidity	Yield	State Taxation	Basis
U.S. Treasury bills (T-bills)	U.S. government obligations	$10,000 to $1 million	Virtually complete	3 and 6 month, sold weekly; 9 month and 1 year, sold monthly	Large active market	Varying recently from 5% to 8%	No	Sold at discount; traded at market value
Federal agency issues	Bonds, notes, and debentures from 6 major federal agencies	Most are $10,000 and up	Considered to be government guaranteed	6 months to 10 years	Large active market	10–40 basis points (0.1% to 0.5%) above T-bills	Varies	Either discounted or interest bearing
Commercial paper	Unsecured interest-bearing notes of large corporations	$25,000 to $5 million	Very high; backed by financially strong corporations	3–270 days	Lack of liquidity	Above T-bills and below bank's prime rate	Yes	Sold at discount
Certificates of deposit (CDs)	Interest-bearing obligations of banks; similar to time deposits but negotiable	$100,000 to $1 million	High to very high; backed by large banks	3 months to 1 year	Active market for large denominations and major banks	Above T-bills; wide variation between different CDs	Yes	Sold at par; interest bearing; traded at market value
Banker's acceptances	Draft instructing bank to pay acceptance holder	$25,000 to $1 million	Very high; backed by 2 or 3 financially strong parties	30–270 days	Market centered in New York	20–50 basis points (0.2% to 0.5%) above T-bills	Yes	Discounted

EXHIBIT 9–1 SURPLUS CASH INVESTMENT OPPORTUNITIES

Exhibit continued on next page.

Exhibit 9–1 Continued from previous page.

Investment	Description	Denominations	Safety	Maturity	Liquidity	Yield	State Taxation	Basis
Repurchase agreements	Agreement by government securities dealer to sell and repurchase securities	$100,000 and up	Very high; government security collateral	1 day or more	None, but the repurchase date can be set in advance to meet the investor's needs	Low but a flexible investment	Yes	Contract
Tax-exempt obligations	Bonds and notes from state and city governments; exempt from federal income tax	$1,000 and up	Ranges from excellent to unacceptable	2 months to several years	Ranges from high to none	Tax exemption can lead to very high effective yield	No, if issued in own state	Usually interest bearing
Money market funds	Private funds pooling investor's money to purchase money market securities	$1,000–$5,000 minimum	Usually high; depends on fund's investments	All investments 1 year or less	Often completely liquid without prior notice	Typically 0% to 0.5% below commercial paper yields	Yes	Sold and redeemed at par; interest bearing
Eurodollar deposits	A time deposit, denominated in dollars in a bank outside the U.S.	$1 million minimum	Very safe	1 day or more	No secondary market	Above domestic CDs	No	Sold at par

The Treasury occasionally sells tax-anticipation bills. Most corporations must pay taxes quarterly in the middle of March, June, September, and December. Tax-anticipation bills mature near these quarterly tax-due dates, and a corporation can use them at full face value to pay taxes. For example, a corporation might know that it has a $2 million tax bill due on March 15. This company could buy tax-anticipation bills that mature in the middle of March and use these notes to pay its taxes when it files its quarterly return.

The Treasury also issues interest-bearing obligations with longer maturities. Treasury bonds have maturities of more than ten years, and notes have maturities of one to ten years. Unlike Treasury bills, these Treasury securities pay interest. If the interest rate printed on the securities is below the current rate on short-term T-bills, these longer-term securities usually sell at a discount. This discount brings the effective interest rate closer to the short-term T-bill rate. The safety and liquidity of these longer-term Treasury securities are fully equal to T-bills.

FEDERAL AGENCY ISSUES

In addition to the Treasury, other federal agencies issue securities. Like T-bills, most of these securities are sold at a discount price that gives an effective return very close to that of T-bills. The same government securities dealers and banks that maintain a secondary market in T-bills also maintain a secondary market in federal agency securities. These issues are *not* a legal debt of the U.S. Treasury and are *not* guaranteed by the government. Because of the close association of these agencies with the government, many people feel that they are government guaranteed. Perhaps because of their slightly higher risk, the short-term issues of federal agencies usually offer a yield that is 10 to 40 basis points higher than the current T-bill rate. A basis point is equal to one-hundredth of a percentage point on an interest rate. The term is used to facilitate the comparison of rates of return on various investments. In the case of short-term issues of federal agencies, 10 to 40 basis points are equivalent to a 0.1 to 0.4 percent higher yield.

There are five principal federal agencies that issue short-term securities:

1. The Federal National Mortgage Association (FNMA or Fannie Mae) buys and sells mortgages guaranteed by the Federal Housing Administration (FHA) and the Veteran's Administration (VA).
2. The Government Mortgage Association (Ginnie Mae) provides mortgage money for homeowners.
3. Federal Land Banks (FLBs) extend long-term credit to Federal Land Bank associations. These associations then make long-term loans to farmers. Typical FLB bonds mature in about ten years.
4. Federal Intermediate Credit Banks (FICBs) sell nine-month debentures each month and then lend the funds to credit associations and agricultural credit corporations.
5. The 13 Banks for Cooperatives (BCs) issue six-month debentures once or twice a month.

COMMERCIAL PAPER

Commercial paper is the popular name for short-term, unsecured promissory notes issued by corporations. Corporate paper is issued by industrial, commercial, financial, and banking corporations. Because commercial paper is unsecured, only the largest and most creditworthy corporations can successfully sell these promissory notes. The maturities on corporate paper range from a few days to nine months, but the most popular maturities are three to six months or nine months. Most commercial paper is sold at a discount and offers an effective interest rate somewhat higher than the current T-bill rate. Corporations occasionally issue commercial paper in denominations as small as $25,000. The denominations for most commercial paper range from $100,000 to $5 million.

Corporations sell their commercial paper either directly to the buyer or to dealers. Only the most financially sound corporations can sell their paper directly, but this route accounts for the largest dollar volume of transactions. Smaller corporations sell their paper through dealers. These dealers carefully investigate the financial strength of all potential issuers. They select only issuers who meet their high standards of size, financial conditions, and reputation.

Because of the large percentage of commercial paper placed directly, there is very little secondary market for commercial paper. Therefore, cash managers should buy commercial paper expecting to hold it to maturity. This makes commercial paper generally unacceptable for the cash backup segment of a company's marketable securities portfolio. However, by selecting the appropriate maturities, a company can safely hold commercial paper in the predictable cash needs or free cash segments of its portfolio. Although the secondary market for commercial paper is small, direct sellers of commercial paper will usually repurchase their paper if requested to do so.

NEGOTIABLE CERTIFICATES OF DEPOSIT

Negotiable certificates of deposit (CDs) are the interest-paying obligations of commercial banks. They are similar to time deposits except that they are negotiable; that is, the original buyer can sell the CD to a third party. A CD proves that the owner has a specified amount of money on deposit at the named bank for a specific period of time and at a specified interest rate. Generally, the maturity of CDs ranges from 30 to 360 days. However, since CDs are negotiable, you can buy them with almost any maturity you want.

CDs offer a greater yield than Treasury bills and roughly the same yield as commercial paper. However, the interest range from the lowest quality to the highest quality CD can be as much as 75 basis points (three-quarters of 1 percent). Three factors determine the quality of a CD:

1. *The size and reputation* of the issuing bank.
2. *The maturity date.* Companies prefer CDs that mature just before monthly and quarterly tax payment dates; thus, because the demand is higher for these CDs, the yield on them is lower.
3. *The denomination.* The most popular denomination is $1 million.

There is a large, deep secondary market for CDs; therefore, substantial holdings may be traded in a single transaction. This makes large denomination CDs very liquid but decreases the liquidity of smaller CDs. In fact, some dealers will not buy CDs in denominations under $500,000, nor will they buy the CDs of smaller banks.

Banks initially sell their CDs at par and offer to pay interest at maturity. If the original buyer then decides to sell the CD, market forces determine the price. The Federal Reserve system uses Regulation Q to control the maximum rate that banks can pay on CDs. Because this regulation does not allow competitive rates for CDs with maturities of less than 90 days, nearly all new CDs are issued with maturities of three months or more.

BANKER'S ACCEPTANCES

A banker's acceptance is a draft that instructs a bank to pay a specified amount of money to the owner of the acceptance at a specified future date. The bank signs the draft in acceptance of its obligation to make this payment. There are four types of banker's acceptances, usually connected with foreign trade:

1. To finance exports or imports.
2. To finance the storage of goods in international trade.
3. To finance the storage of goods in domestic trade.
4. To facilitate foreign currency exchanges.

Banker's acceptances are considered very safe because almost everyone connected with them is responsible for their ultimate payment. Primary responsibility rests with the accepting bank, of course, but the original maker (often a foreign trader) is also responsible. Furthermore, if a dealer buys the acceptance from the bank and later sells it to an investor, the dealer is also responsible in case of default by the bank or the original maker.

The standard maturity on banker's acceptances is 90 days. Because acceptances are actively traded, an investor can usually purchase an acceptance on the open market with any needed maturity less than 90 days. Bond dealers and many large banks maintain a market in banker's acceptances, and this provides excellent liquidity. Banker's acceptances typically yield 20 to 50 basis points (0.2 to 0.5 percent) above the prevailing T-bill rate.

REPURCHASE AGREEMENTS

A repurchase agreement is a contract between a government security dealer and an investor (usually a corporation). The government security dealer sells U.S. Treasury securities (or other securities) to the investor and simultaneously agrees to repurchase those securities for a specified price on a specified future date. In this way, government securities dealers can finance large inventories of government securities, and investors can get an essentially risk-free investment with any maturity they choose, with a yield approximately equal to CDs. The three basic types of repurchase agreements are:

1. *Overnight transaction.* The investor purchases the securities one day, and the dealer repurchases them the following day.
2. *Open repurchase transaction.* The investor purchases the securities and holds them until either party (investor or dealer) calls for a repurchase.
3. *Fixed date repurchase transaction.* The investor knows in advance the date of his or her cash requirement and specifies the repurchase date in advance.

Repurchase agreements have virtually no secondary market. Consequently, companies enter into repurchase agreements only when they can accurately plan their cash needs in advance.

TAX-EXEMPT OBLIGATIONS

City and state governments and their agencies can issue bonds on which the interest is exempt from U.S. income tax. For an investor in the 34 percent tax bracket (most corporations, for example), tax-exempt interest is worth slightly more than one and a half times its stated value. For instance, if a company invests $100,000 in an 8 percent taxable bond, it earns $8,000 in a year and must pay $2,720 in federal tax, leaving $5,280 net profit. On the other hand, if the company invests the same $100,000 in a 6 percent tax-exempt security, it receives $6,000 in one year but pays no federal tax and is thus left with the full $6,000. In this case, the 6 percent tax-exempt security supplies a greater net profit than the 8 percent taxable security.

The creditworthiness of tax-exempt securities ranges from excellent to unacceptable. You can find estimates of the credit risk of tax-exempt obligations in standard bond rating tables, such as those prepared by Moody's or Standard and Poor's. The liquidity of tax-exempt obligations ranges from very good to none at all.

MONEY MARKET FUNDS

When interest rates on 90-day commercial paper and CDs rise substantially, many smaller investors want to obtain these high yields but do not have the $100,000 minimum investment necessary to purchase most of these investments. To meet this need, several investment companies formed money market funds that pooled the smaller investments of thousands of investors and then purchased short-term money market instruments.

Money market funds offer several advantages to investors:

1. *Low minimum investment.* A typical investment is $1,000 to $5,000.
2. *Complete liquidity.* In most funds, investors can withdraw at will.
3. *Relatively high safety.* Most funds invest in a wide variety of very safe securities. The variety of investments also helps decrease the risk by eliminating the investors' dependence on a small number of securities.
4. *High yield.* The money market funds can afford to buy the high denomination ($1 million and up) investments that offer the highest

yields. In addition, by buying in large quantities, commissions as a percentage of transaction size are reduced. The fund itself, however, adds its own service charges that offset some of these savings.

5. *Convenience*. Professional money managers make all investment decisions, thus relieving the individual investor or small company cash manager of this job.

In this way, money market funds allow smaller companies to earn a high return on their surplus funds, just as very large corporations do.

Unfortunately, many portfolio managers overestimate the complexity of money market trading. They believe that only an experienced Wall Street financier can buy and sell CDs, banker's acceptances, and repurchase agreements. In fact, whatever can be done on Wall Street can be done in any major city of the country.

The easiest and safest way for a company to buy money market securities is through the investment department of the company's bank. The larger banks in all large cities have money market departments that are fully prepared to purchase whatever securities you want. Alternatively, a cash manager can buy securities directly. For example, a company can purchase commercial paper directly from several large corporations and finance companies. General Motors Acceptance Corporation and Household Finance Corporation both issue commercial paper directly. The aggressive cash manager can purchase CDs and banker's acceptances directly from issuing banks. In addition, many brokerage firms will assist a cash manager with a purchase of money market securities.

EURODOLLAR DEPOSITS

Eurodollars are deposits denominated in dollars in banks or foreign branches of U.S. banks outside the United States. These banks are not under the jurisdiction of the Federal Reserve, so they can issue time deposits that are not allowed in the United States, at rates not subject to Federal Reserve regulations. The market is largely a wholesale market, and Eurobanks will accept deposits from well-known corporations, banks, and governments. A unique feature of the Euromarket is that, because of the myriad of nationalities, financial practices, and varying degrees of information disclosure, an informal channel of information has emerged. For these reasons, depositors tend to place their money with the largest and best known Eurobanks rather than with the smaller, more obscure banks. This has helped reduce the riskiness of the investment.

➤ OTHER INVESTMENT OPTIONS FOR SURPLUS CASH

In recent years, there have been two major innovations in preferred stock investments: adjustable-rate preferred stock (ARPs) and Dutch Auction preferred issues. Since 80 percent of preferred dividends are exempt from federal income taxation, these securities are more attractive than traditional money market securities. Moreover, since these securities provide both high after-tax yields and price stability, they are favored by investors over traditional preferred stock. Although both ARPs and Dutch Auction preferred issues have a floating dividend rate and provide corporate investors with a dividend exclusion, the two categories of issues differ in how the dividend is set. We discuss these differences below.

The dividend rate on adjustable rate preferred stock is adjusted quarterly to the highest of the 90-day Treasury bill rate, the 10-year Treasury note rate, or the 20-year Treasury bond rate. The quarterly dividend is expressed in terms of a spread above or below the appropriate Treasury yield, which is termed the reset. ARPs also have collars that specify maximum and minimum dividend levels. When the prices of the instruments hit the collar, the issues take on the characteristics of a fixed rate preferred instrument.

ADJUSTABLE RATE PREFERRED STOCK

Only a limited number of issuers have taken advantage of this market. In addition, the primary and secondary markets for the issues are quite narrow since the demand for ARPs comes primarily from institutional investors. Therefore, if a treasurer must liquidate a position quickly, the limited nature of the investment base could exacerbate the price impact.

Corporate investors in ARPs must be concerned with the strength of the issuer and the industry group. Because of these concerns about the credit quality of the issuers, the ARPs market has not performed as well as early supporters had hoped. As a result of many issues selling below par, a new instrument, the Dutch Auction rate preferred stock, was developed.

The dividend rate for Dutch Auction issues is not set by the issuer but through the following process: Every 49 days (seven weeks) bidders submit an offer for a specified number of shares at the lowest dividend yield they are willing to accept. The lowest dividend yield that is bid and results in all the shares being sold becomes the prevailing yield for the next seven weeks. Existing investors who already own shares have the option to keep their shares at the prevailing dividend yield, or they can bid a lower rate and risk losing their shares to a lower bidder. Typically, the dividend rate for Dutch Auction preferred issues is at 60 to 80 percent of the 60-day rate on commercial paper.

DUTCH AUCTION PREFERRED STOCK

From the viewpoint of the corporate investor, these securities have some advantages over ARPs. First, the 49-day reset period on the Dutch Auction issues is shorter than the 90-day period found in the ARPs market. Consequently, Dutch Auction issues experience less price volatility than ARPs. Moreover, the shorter reset period offers the corporate treasurer greater liquidity if funds are needed for operating activities. The Dutch Auction procedure also makes it more likely that the issue will sell at par. However, investors in Dutch Auction issues are exposed to the same credit quality risks that exist with adjustable rate preferred issues. In addition, the auction could fail if there are not enough bids to match offers to sell. In this case, the dividend rate for the subsequent 49-day period is set by a fixed formula.

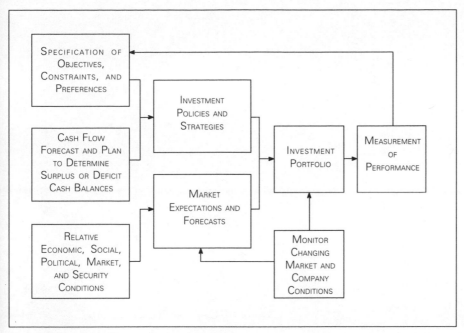

EXHIBIT 9–2   CASH SURPLUS INVESTING PROCESS

The idea of investing surplus cash can be viewed as a process, where we define a process as an integrated set of activities that combine in a logical, orderly manner to achieve a desired outcome. Each individual money manager may adapt the process to fit his or her individual needs and preferences, however, the structure remains the same. In Exhibit 9–2 we present the basic framework for investing cash surplus.

➤ SUMMARY

When corporations have surplus cash to invest, the cash manager must carefully evaluate the safety, liquidity, and yield of each investment. Investment possibilities include bank savings accounts and the nine principal money market investments (U.S. Treasury securities; federal agency issues; commercial paper; certificates of deposit; banker's acceptances; repurchase agreements; tax-exempt obligations; money market funds, which make it possible for smaller companies to invest in money instruments offering higher yields; and Eurodollar deposits).

In addition to money market investments, there are two preferred stock investments that are favored by corporate investors. Adjustable-rate preferred stocks (ARPs) and Dutch Auction preferred issues offer the added attraction of dividends that are partially exempt from federal income taxation.

The excess cash investing process starts with gathering information about the company, its environment, and money markets. This information is used to make investment decisions in forming a portfolio of many market instruments. A necessary part of the process is the feedback and monitor activity, which is used to revise the size and composition of the investment portfolio given changing conditions in the markets or the company.

CHAPTER 10

INTERNATIONAL
CASH MANAGEMENT

By the end of this chapter, the reader will be able to:

1. Differentiate between the spot and the forward market.
2. Describe the two basic instruments for financing foreign trade.
3. Discuss the types of foreign banks and the services they offer.
4. Discuss the characteristics of foreign investments.
5. Be familiar with the systems used for international payment.

Managing cash, marketable securities, accounts receivable, and inventory is always a complex situation; it is significantly more complex for multinational corporations. One basic problem is that business conducted in foreign countries must be transacted in the local currency. In any international transaction, dollars must be converted to the local currency and back again. In this chapter, we look first at the process of foreign exchange. Next, we discuss the ways in which foreign trade is financed. Then, because foreign banks can assist corporations, we describe briefly the services offered by international banks and bankers, including both foreign-owned banks and the foreign branches of U.S. banks. Finally, we discuss foreign investment opportunities, including interest rates, taxes, and restrictions on remittances to the United States, and centralized versus decentralized cash management.

➢ FOREIGN EXCHANGE

More than 150 local currencies are in use throughout the world. These include U.S. dollars, British pounds, French francs, German marks, Saudi Arabian riyals, Indian rupees, Japanese yen, and Chilean escudos. When you conduct business in a foreign country, you will almost always use the local currency. Therefore, when your business involves transactions in two or more countries, you will usually have to exchange one currency for another. For example, suppose that an American company wants to make an investment in Italy. The American company will have to exchange its dollars for Italian lire and then use the lire to make the Italian investment. As another example, suppose that a company in Bolivia wants to buy farm equipment from an American company. The Bolivian company will first have to change its pesos into dollars and then use the dollars to purchase the equipment from the company in America.

Different currencies have different values. For example, you can buy ten rupees in Nepal with one U.S. dollar, but you will need $.27 to buy one riyal in Saudi Arabia. The relative values of currencies fluctuate a small amount (1 to 2 percent) every day and may change 10 or 20 percent or more over a few months.

The foreign exchange market is not located in one place; rather, it is a communication network of telephones and telexes connecting large commercial banks and the central banks of the world. Usually, a corporation wishing to purchase or sell foreign exchange will do so through a commercial bank.

Spot Market

The simplest way to exchange currency is on the spot market. You simply give the money you want to exchange to a bank (or other foreign exchange agent) and immediately receive in return the equivalent amount of money in the currency of your choice (minus a brokerage fee). Actually, you do not have to use cash in a transaction of this type; it can all be handled either by check or by transferring money from a bank in one country to a bank in another country.

The cost of this exchange service varies with the currencies involved and the size of the transaction. Among major currencies (dollars, pounds, francs, marks, and yen), the exchange cost is a small fraction of 1 percent of the transaction amount. For minor currencies or currencies threatened by devaluation, the exchange cost may be several percent of the transaction amount.

Because foreign exchange rates fluctuate, a buyer of foreign goods always takes a risk when agreeing to pay a specified amount in a foreign currency on a future date. For example, suppose that your company decides to buy a German printing press for 500,000 marks. Suppose that when you sign the purchase order in July, the mark is valued at $0.40; you would, therefore, expect the press to cost $200,000 (500,000 marks × $0.40 per mark). However, if the printing press is installed in October and the value of the mark has risen to $0.42 at that time, your company will have to pay $210,000 (500,000 marks × $0.42 per mark). This extra $10,000 in cost is due solely to the rise in the value of the German mark between the time you placed the order and the time you paid the bill. (Of course, if the mark had dropped to $0.38 during that time, your company would have saved $10,000.)

Many companies do not like to be exposed to the risk of foreign exchange rate fluctuations. Therefore, they may buy the 500,000 marks at the same time that they place the order and hold the marks in a bank until the bill comes due. This guarantees that the press will cost them $200,000, regardless of any fluctuations in the exchange rate between the dollar and the mark.

There is another solution for companies that do not wish to tie up their capital for several months in a foreign currency. This is the *forward market*. The forward market allows you to buy a contract for delivery of a specified amount of a foreign currency on a specified date. For example, you might buy 500,000 German marks for October delivery at a net price of $0.40 per mark. No matter how much the value of the mark rises between July and October, you will be able to buy 500,000 marks for $200,000.

Another way of ensuring that the exchange rate on the date of the transaction is fixed is to use currency options. An option is a financial instrument that gives the holder the right, but not the obligation, to buy (call) or sell (put) a specific amount of a foreign currency at a fixed price during a specific period. The writer of the put or call option must fulfill the contract if the buyer so desires. The right to buy or sell at your choice has some value, and this value is reflected in the premium or price paid for the option.

The cost of such a contract varies with market expectations of future fluctuations in exchange rates. This contract might cost $5,000, which can be considered insurance against a possible rise in the value of the mark. However, you do not have to exercise your option in October. If the value of the mark falls to $0.36, you can let your option expire and buy the marks you need for $180,000 (500,000 marks × $0.36 per mark). Therefore, an option contract of this type insures you against loss if the value of the foreign currency rises but still allows you to take advantage of any drop in the value of the foreign currency.

The Chicago Mercantile Exchange began trading futures contracts on foreign currencies in 1972. The International Money Market (IMM) division of the Merc trades futures contracts for the British pound, Canadian dollar, Deutsche mark, Swiss franc, French franc, Japanese yen, Australian dollar, and European Currency Unit. The London International Financial Futures Exchange (LIFFE) began operations in 1982. Currencies such as pounds, marks, francs, and yen are traded on the LIFFE.

The currency futures contracts are agreements to buy or sell a specific amount of a given currency; the exchange rate is fixed at the time the contract is originated, and the delivery date is determined by the exchange (i.e., IMM or LIFFE). The contracts can be bought and sold by paying a commission of as little as $15 for the more actively traded contracts.

In addition to using the forward options or futures markets, a company has other alternatives to protect itself against foreign exchange rate fluctuations. For example, the company can hedge its monetary position by offsetting monetary assets—such as cash and accounts receivables—with monetary liabilities—such as payables. If a change in exchange rates occurs, the monetary assets and liabilities change by the same amount, and therefore the net monetary position of the firm, is unaffected. Alternatively, the firm could enter into a foreign currency swap arrangement whereby two parties agree to exchange one currency for another at a specified future date and exchange ratio. Parallel loans are similar in concept to swaps. In these transactions, a bank arranges for two parent companies to lend to each other's subsidiary in their own countries. Finally, the company can adjust intercompany accounts by transferring funds from a sub-

FORWARD MARKET

sidiary with a weakening currency to a subsidiary whose currency is expected to appreciate.

➤ FINANCING
FOREIGN TRADE

Importing and exporting goods and services are the most important forms of international commerce. In many ways, buying from or selling to a company in another country is similar to buying and selling within national boundaries. However, foreign transactions are more complex because two currencies are usually involved, two countries' laws must be considered, and communication is often slow and expensive.

The two basic instruments of foreign trade financing are bank drafts and letters of credit. Two less frequently used transactions are sales on open account and cash in advance.

Bank drafts, or bills of exchange, allow exporters to use their bank as the collection agent for foreign accounts. The bank forwards the exporter's invoices to the foreign buyer, either directly by mail or through a branch or correspondent bank in the buyer's country. When the buyer pays the draft, the exporter's bank converts the proceeds of the collection into the exporter's currency and deposits this money in the exporter's account.

BANK DRAFTS

A sight draft is payable on presentation to the importer, and the exporter usually receives the proceeds within one or two weeks. Normally, the exporter's bank (or its correspondent bank) in the buyer's country does not present the draft for payment by the importer until the merchandise has actually arrived (usually by ship). When the importer (buyer) has verified that all paperwork is in order and that the goods have arrived, the importer pays the bank and receives title to the merchandise.

In addition to sight drafts, which are payable on presentation, time drafts are frequently drawn; these specify that payment is required in 30, 60, or 90 days, or more. With a time draft, the title to the merchandise is delivered when the buyer promises to pay rather than when the buyer actually pays the bill.

To minimize the risk involved in foreign trade, an exporter may require the buyer to open a letter of credit at a specified bank. Sometimes, buyers will obtain a letter of credit under their own incentive to obtain more favorable treatment by the exporter. A letter of credit is a guarantee by the buyer's bank to a seller to honor the seller's drafts that are drawn on the bank, provided that the drafts comply with the terms specified in the letter of credit and are accompanied by the necessary documents.

LETTERS OF CREDIT

A letter of credit works in the following way: First, the buyer requests the bank to create a letter of credit in favor of the seller. Second, the bank creates the letter of credit and informs its foreign correspondent bank in the seller's country that it has done so. Then, the correspondent bank in the seller's country notifies the seller about the credit. Next, the seller ships the goods to the buyer and receives a bill of lading from the shipper. (The bill of lading is a shipping document used to transport the exporter's goods to the importer.) The seller submits the invoices and the bill of lading to the correspondent bank. The bank, in turn, verifies the paperwork and pays the seller. Then the correspondent bank sends the paperwork to the buyer's bank. Next, the buyer's bank pays the correspondent bank and sends the documents to the buyer, who makes the payment. The buyer sends the bill of lading to the shipper and receives the merchandise in return.

A letter of credit provides three important benefits to importers:

1. In cases where prepayment is required, importers are safer if they deposit money with their own bank rather than with the seller in a foreign country. Then, if the seller does not ship the goods, it is relatively easy for buyers to recover deposits from their own bank.
2. In cases where prepayment is not required, buyers can finance their purchase through their own bank at a relatively low cost.
3. Buyers are able to bargain for a lower price and better terms from the seller because they have substituted the bank's credit for their own. Since buyers who obtain a letter of credit have eliminated most of the risk for the seller, they are justified in asking for lower prices and better terms.

Letters of credit also offer substantial advantages to exporters. The exporter receives payment immediately after shipping the merchandise if the letter of credit specifies sight drafts. In cases where the letter of credit calls for time drafts, the exporter receives a note from a bank (banker's acceptance) rather than a note from the buyer, and this bank note is virtually risk free. Another advantage to letters of credit is that the seller reduces his or her risk to foreign exchange rate fluctuations because the seller is paid quickly.

SALES ON OPEN ACCOUNT

Bank drafts (bills of exchange) and letters of credit are the two most common forms of transacting foreign trade; both approaches have many variations. Exporters may also sell on open account or require cash in advance. Sales on open account are the least complex of all foreign trade transactions. The seller simply ships the goods to the buyer, sends an invoice to the buyer, and waits for payment. Although this approach is simple, the seller assumes all the risks of foreign exchange fluctuations, currency remittance restrictions (by the buyer's government), and buyer default or bankruptcy. Because of this, exporters generally extend open account terms only to their most reliable customers in economically stable countries.

CASH IN ADVANCE

At the other extreme, some exporters may require cash in advance. In this case, the buyer must pay in full before the goods are shipped. This, obviously, fully protects the seller. Here, the buyer assumes all the risks of foreign exchange fluctuations and seller default or bankruptcy.

➤ Foreign Banking

To do business with companies in foreign countries, it is usually necessary to have a bank in that country. This may be a foreign branch of a U.S. bank, a correspondent bank, or a completely autonomous foreign bank.

The largest U.S. banks have branch offices in foreign countries. For example, the Chase Manhattan Bank and Citibank in New York have foreign branch offices. So do Bank of America and the First National Bank of Boston. In general, foreign branches of U.S. banks are almost self-contained banks and are complete with departments for foreign and domestic operations. Originally, the foreign branches of U.S. banks primarily served the local subsidiaries of U.S. companies, but now many foreign branches also serve foreign-owned companies in the country where they are located.

TYPES OF
FOREIGN BANKS

More commonly, U.S. banks have correspondent banks in foreign countries. These correspondent banks are owned and managed by citizens of the foreign country but are closely associated with a specific U.S. bank. This arrangement allows a U.S. bank to have a close working relationship with literally hundreds of foreign banks in cities throughout the world. This network enables a U.S. company to do business quickly and easily almost anywhere in the world. Approximately 95 percent of foreign banking by U.S. companies is done with correspondent banks.

Finally, some companies prefer to do business with completely independent foreign banks. This is not normally done, however. (Occasionally, a U.S. company will do business with an independent foreign bank if, for some reason, the transaction can be controlled more easily using that bank.)

Foreign banks—whether branches of U.S. banks, correspondent banks, or independent foreign banks—offer a wide variety of services to any company doing business internationally. These services include providing letters of introduction to foreign bankers, businesspersons, and government officials; exchanging money, both in the spot market and in the forward market; financing foreign trade (through loans or overdrafts); providing credit information on both exporters and importers; handling international payments and collections, primarily through drafts (bills of exchange) and letters of credit; providing advice on foreign trade and trade development; providing advice on mergers and acquisitions; offering publications on domestic and international economic, business, and financial conditions; and offering cash mobilization systems that reduce the amount of idle cash building up in company accounts anywhere in the world.

SERVICES OF
INTERNATIONAL
BANKS AND BANKERS

Banks charge for many of these international services, and the charges vary significantly from country to country. Furthermore, banks involved in international transactions frequently require substantial deposits in noninterest-bearing accounts. These funds give the bank additional income and simultaneously provide security either for the customer's letter of credit or for loans against collections.

➤ FOREIGN INVESTMENTS

Many of the same types of investments that are available in the United States are also available in foreign countries. For example, a company can deposit money in a bank savings account and earn interest. Similarly, the company can buy bonds (either corporate or government) in most foreign countries. Corporate stocks are sold on an organized market in most of the larger foreign countries. In addition, a company may invest in assets in the foreign country, including inventories, real estate, and buildings.

The primary risk involved in foreign financial investments (bank accounts, bonds, and stock) is the devaluation of the foreign currency. For example, assume that a U.S. company's Mexican subsidiary could remit the money to the parent company in the United States or reinvest the pesos in a Mexican bank if it believes that the returns are attractive in Mexico. However, if the Mexican government significantly devalues the peso, the value of the U.S. company's Mexican assets would decline dramatically. In recent years, several South American countries, including Mexico, Brazil, and Argentina, have devalued their currencies in response to accelerating inflation rates. On the other hand, foreign currencies may be revalued (increased in value), or the dollar may be devalued. In this case, individuals or companies holding money in a foreign currency may come out ahead. For example, the Japanese yen appreciated approximately 85 percent against the U.S. dollar between July 1985 and July 1988.

Holding assets, such as inventory, land, or buildings, does not expose the owner to foreign exchange rate fluctuations because, as the exchange rate changes, the value of the assets also changes. However, holding material assets in a foreign country does expose the owner to risks like nationalization and other forms of expropriation. This risk varies widely from country to country; it is very small in most European countries, but it can be quite high in some South American and Asian countries.

RISKS

Bank deposit rates and other interest rates vary primarily according to the country's rate of inflation and its domestic tranquillity. Of course, the rates also vary over time as conditions change. These days, the rates vary from about 3 percent (for certain Swiss bank accounts) to about 15 to 20 percent (in countries with high, but not uncontrolled, inflation rates and some political instability).

DEPOSIT AND INTEREST RATES

Most foreign countries impose taxes on their own citizens and on foreign companies doing business within their boundaries. These taxes are usually on net income, net sales, or assets. Occasionally, there is a minimum tax. Some countries charge the same rates for both their own citizens and foreign companies, whereas other countries charge different rates to different groups. Some of these other countries charge higher rates to foreign companies in order to encourage local ownership and increase the flow of tax

TAXES

revenue into their countries. Other countries charge lower rates to foreign companies (such as complete immunity from all taxes for ten years) in order to encourage foreign investment in their countries and to create jobs and build up the local economy.

The U.S. government allows American companies to deduct part or all of their foreign tax payments as a legitimate business expense. However, the rules governing the tax credits vary (depending on the specific situation) and change fairly frequently.

In addition to imposing taxes on companies, foreign governments may restrict the flow of capital out of their territories. A corporation can repatriate funds by any of the following means: dividends, interest and loan repayment, royalties, management fees, and payments for goods and services provided by the parent company. The host government may limit or bar any or all of these methods of repatriation. Additionally, the tax implications of repatriated funds in the United States must be considered. Therefore, before investing in a foreign country or repatriating earnings from an established foreign investment, a U.S. corporation should investigate both the current and future restrictions on remittances to the United States.

RESTRICTIONS ON
REMITTANCES TO THE
UNITED STATES

The external money and capital markets—that is, financial markets that are not subject to the regulations of any one country—provide both sources of funds and investment opportunities in the international arena. The Eurodollar market provides investment opportunities in the form of time deposits and commercial paper. Firms and governments can borrow from Eurobanks for short-term as well as intermediate-term needs. The Eurobond market is the external long-term market, where funds denominated in various currencies are gathered and made available to borrowers without any regulation by national governments. There are investment opportunities available for those who desire longer-term investments, and funds are made available to those seeking long-term financing.

INTERNATIONAL
MONEY AND
CAPITAL MARKETS

These external markets will exist as long as national authorities try artificially to regulate, control, and allocate financing in their own countries. And, in fact, it is believed that, even if all capital controls were abolished, the Euromarkets would continue to exist because they have the momentum to continue even though the reason for their existence is removed.

➤ CENTRALIZED VERSUS
DECENTRALIZED CASH MANAGEMENT

A firm's cash management system can be either centralized or decentralized on a company level. A decentralized system permits subsidiaries to use surplus cash in any way they desire. In a centralized cash management system, however, each subsidiary holds at the local level the minimum cash balance required for transactions purposes. All funds not needed for transactions purposes are then forwarded to a central cash center. Although the managers of local subsidiaries often prefer a decentralized cash management system, a centralized approach has several advantages. First, a centralized system allows for netting, which reduces the transaction costs for payments between subsidiaries and permits intersubsidiary cash flows to be forecast more accurately. In a netting system, a single net payment is made instead of separate payments for each amount owed between subsidiaries. Second, a centralized cash center is able to collect information more quickly regarding the strengths and weaknesses of various currencies. In addition, it can increase the yields on short-term investments by pooling the excess cash of the company's subsidiaries. Third, funds held in a centralized cash center can be returned to a subsidiary facing a cash shortage via a wire transfer. The central pool of funds eliminates the possibility that a subsidiary will borrow funds locally at high interest rates while another unit invests surplus funds at a low rate. As a result of these advantages, most multinational corporations have adopted a centralized cash management system.

➤ International Payment Systems

A number of clearing and settlement systems have developed over time to initiate and complete payment for international transactions. A comparison of these systems follows.

FED WIRE

The Fed Wire is operated by the Federal Reserve System, and is limited to U.S. dollar-denominated transactions initiated and received in the United States. Since Fed Wire transfers are guaranteed by the U.S. government, liquidity and credit risks are minimized for the users of the system.

CLEARING HOUSE INTERBANK PAYMENT SYSTEM (CHIPS)

CHIPS is a private payment clearing system located in New York City and operated by the New York Clearing House Association. It is a dollar-denominated network specializing in international payments. It is estimated that 90 percent of all international interbank dollar transactions are transferred through CHIPS. A comparison of the activity on CHIPS and the Fed Wire is shown in Exhibit 10–1.

CLEARING HOUSE AUTOMATED PAYMENT SYSTEM (CHAPS)

CHAPS is a large-value electronic credit transfer system providing same-day value for British pound payments. Located in London, the clearing network is similar to CHIPS. There are 14 CHAPS members that operate the system and settle at the end of the day through the Bank of England. Transfer services are made available to other banks and customers through these 14 members.

The growth of CHAPS is shown in Exhibit 10–2. Transfers through CHAPS are considered final in that they are guaranteed, irrevocable, and

	CHIPS		Fed Wire	
	NUMBER OF TRANSACTIONS	DOLLAR AMOUNT	NUMBER OF TRANSACTIONS	DOLLAR AMOUNT
Securities purchase/ redemption/ financing	274	$ 2,842	4,458	$ 54,856
Bank loan	399	3,476	272	3,956
Federal funds	107	788	3,361	66,269
Commercial and miscellaneous	1,295	12,793	2,690	33,593
Settlement	945	16,198	915	18,664
Eurodollar placement	4,800	56,255	966	18,848
Foreign exchange	20,674	112,505	173	858
Total	28,494	$204,857	11,836	$197,043

EXHIBIT 10–1   FINANCIAL TRANSACTIONS THROUGH CHIPS AND FED WIRE BY TYPE OF TRANSACTION ($ MILLIONS).   (Estimated aggregate transactions based on subsample survey.) Source: "Large-Dollar Payment Flows from New York," FRB-NY Quarterly Review, Federal Reserve Bank of New York (Winter 1987–88).

unconditional. However, it must be remembered that this is a private system, and thus the transfers are guaranteed by the members and not the Bank of England.

THE BANK OF JAPAN NETWORK SYSTEM (BOJ-NET)

As the Japanese banks have become increasingly more important in international financial flows, their transfer systems have also grown in importance. The Bank of Japan Financial Network System is a cash and securities wire transfer system. BOJ-NET limits transactions to yen-denominated payments. The cash wire is an on-line funds transfer system for banks and is the Japanese counterpart of CHIPS.

Financial institutions use BOJ-NET to provide net settlement services for the clearing house system that clears bills and checks. It also provides settlement for the Japanese EFT system called Zenguin. The institutions can also use BOJ-NET to settle yen payments that arise from cross-border transfers and foreign exchange transactions.

OTHER SYSTEMS

U.S.-based banks (including Chase Manhattan and Bank of America) operate offshore dollar clearing systems. The most important of these sys-

YEAR	VOLUME (000s)	VALUE (MILLIONS)	AVERAGE TRANSFER VALUE
1984	1,149	$ 741,273	$ 645,146
1985	2,217	2,355,565	1,062,501
1986	3,161	4,143,877	1,310,939
1987	4,386	7,331,906	1,671,661
1988	5,781	11,288,501	1,952,690
1989	7,000	15,500,000	—

EXHIBIT 10–2 CHAPS VOLUME IN BRITISH POUNDS. Source: *Allsopp, Peter, "Large Value Payments Systems: CHAPS and the Town Clearing,"* Payment Systems Worldwide *(Washington, D.C.: Federal Reserve Board of Governor, 1990).*

tems, Chase-Tokyo, serves financial institutions in Japan wishing to clear dollar-yen foreign exchange transactions, the dollar call money market in Tokyo, commercial transactions denominated in dollars, and any Japanese company's payment instruction that requires same-day value for settling dollar transactions. The dollar trading occurs during the Japanese business day with Chase keeping a running tally of positions. The end-of-the-day (in Japan) positions are sent to Chase New York at 3:00 A.M. EST, and then entered into the CHIPS for payment or receipt.

SOCIETY FOR WORLDWIDE INTERBANK FINANCIAL TELECOMMUNICATIONS (SWIFT)

SWIFT is not a settlement system, but a communications system that facilitates settlement of wire transfers through banks in different countries. Currently there are over 1,600 member banks, with most of the membership either in the United States or Europe. The innovative feature of SWIFT is the standardization of messages so that computer software can read SWIFT messages on a worldwide basis. All types of customer and bank transfers are sent through the SWIFT network.

INTERNATIONALIZATION OF AUTOMATED TELLER MACHINES (ATM)

The globalization of automated teller machines is one of the newer examples of the expansion of U.S. financial networks. This system is based on a number of switching networks (each one owned by a different bank or group of banks) that operate on a worldwide basis.

A global ATM network works like a computerized constellation of switches. Each separate bank is part of a regional, national, and international financial system. Exhibit 10–3 shows how a common transaction could be routed through the system. After the customer inserts the credit card, punches a personal identification number, and enters the transaction request, the bank's computer decides that this is not one of its own credit cards, and switches to a national computer. The national computer also does not recognize this card as one of its own, so it switches to an international switch, which routes the request to the U.S. Global Switching Center. At this point, the request is sent to a regional computer in the United States, which evaluates the request and sends a response back

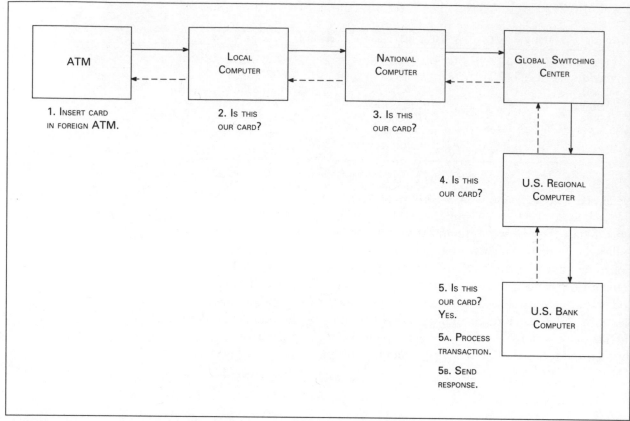

EXHIBIT 10–3   GLOBAL ATM NETWORK

through the switching network. The entire time of the process (from initiation at the ATM until the response is received) is measured in seconds.

The use, acceptance, and growth of systems such as this will revolutionize the way international payments are to be made well into the 21st century.

➤ SUMMARY

To conduct international business, a company must usually handle the currencies of both its own country and the foreign country. Therefore, it must convert money from one currency to another; it can do this on both the spot (current) market and the forward market. Most foreign exchange transactions expose companies to risks of fluctuations in foreign exchange rates. These risks can be reduced by purchasing outright or by negotiating a contract for future delivery of the currency at a specified rate.

In this chapter, we looked at the two principal ways of handling foreign trade: bank drafts (bills of exchange) and letters of credit. Bank drafts allow the seller's bank (or correspondent bank) to collect payments from the buyer and remit these payments to the seller. Letters of credit offer the seller protection against default by the buyer and against most fluctuations in currency exchange rates. Because they give the seller these advantages, a buyer using a letter of credit can frequently negotiate lower prices or better terms. We also looked briefly at two other methods of financing foreign trade: sales on open account and cash in advance.

We discussed foreign banks, including the foreign branches of U.S. banks, correspondent banks, and foreign-owned banks. We saw that international banks and bankers offer a variety of services, including information, advice, letters of introduction, currency exchange, international payment and collection systems, and foreign trade financing.

A wide variety of foreign investments are available, including bank deposits, bonds, and stocks. The principal risks of most foreign investments are devaluation and expropriation. Interest rates vary widely, depending on the country's relative inflation rate and political stability. Finally, we saw that most foreign countries tax the income or assets of companies within their borders; they may also restrict the remittance of profits to the parent company if it is located in another country.

BIBLIOGRAPHY

ALTMAN, EDWARD (ED.). *HANDBOOK OF CORPORATE FIINANCE*. NEW YORK: JOHN WILEY & SONS, 1986.

BREALY, RICHARD A., AND STEWART C. MYERS. *PRINCIPLES OF CORPORATE FINANCE*. NEW YORK: McGRAW-HILL, 1988.

BRIGHAM, EUGENE F., AND LOUIS C. GAPENSKI. *FINANCIAL MANAGEMENT: THEORY AND PRACTICE*, 5TH ED. HINSDALE, ILL: THE DRYDEN PRESS, 1988.

GALLINGER, GEORGE W., AND P. BASIL HEALEY. *LIQUIDITY ANALYSIS AND MANAGEMENT*. READING, MASS.: ADDISON-WESLEY, 1987.

HAMPTON, JOHN J., AND CECILIA L. WAGNER. *WORKING CAPITAL MANAGEMENT*. NEW YORK: JOHN WILEY & SONS, 1989.

HILL, NED C., AND WILLIAM L. SARTORIS. *SHORT-TERM FINANCIAL MANAGEMENT*. NEW YORK: MACMILLAN, 1988.

LEE, CHENG F., AND JOSEPH E. FINNERTY. *CORPORATE FINANCE: THEORY, METHOD, & APPLICATIONS*. SAN DIEGO: HARCOURT BRACE JOVANOVICH, 1990.

LOGUE, DENNIS E. (ED.). *HANDBOOK OF MODERN FINANCE*. BOSTON: WARREN, GORHAM & LAMONT, 1990.

SCHERR, FREDERICK C. *MODERN WORKING CAPITAL MANAGEMENT*. ENGLEWOOD CLIFFS, N.J.: PRENTICE-HALL, 1989.

SHAPIRO, ALAN C. *MULTINATIONAL FINANCIAL MANAGEMENT*. BOSTON: ALLYN & BACON, 1989.

Vander Weide, James, and Steven F. Maier. Managing Corporate Liquidity: An Introduction to Working Capital Management. New York: John Wiley & Sons, 1985.

INDEX